God and the Future

Henry McKeating

GOD AND THE FUTURE

———

SCM PRESS LTD

334 00567 1

First published 1974
by SCM Press Ltd
56 Bloomsbury Street London

© SCM Press Ltd 1974

Printed in Great Britain by
Billing & Sons Ltd
Guildford and London

CONTENTS

1

Man and his Future - The Blessing and Curse of Knowledge

Let me begin with a word of . . . What? I don't know whether it is apology or simply explanation. I find theology difficult; interesting, but difficult. I find it hard to read, hard to talk about, and hard to think about. (It hasn't always been like that. I used to think I coped with theology pretty well, but the more I do the harder it seems to get.)

So if it seems to you that at some points I am trying to deal with theology in words of one syllable, please don't take this as an insult. I'm doing it not to accommodate you, but to accommodate me. The danger, of course, is of superficiality and naïvety. I hope I don't fall into that. There is enough instant theology around.

There is no particular reason why we should *expect* theology to be easy. I have no sympathy with those who claim that faith is intellectually easy, and complain that only theologians and unbelievers make it difficult. Theology is, after all, about God (or at least, it always used to be), and if God is really God (Wholly Other, *Mysterium Tremendum* and all that sort of thing) then you wouldn't expect to find him specially easy to talk

1

about. But on the other hand, if God is what Christians have always claimed, and has spent the better part of human history to date in revealing himself to men, then the things of God must be communicable. Whether it is easy or not, it must be possible to talk about him *somehow.*

Theology is not like most kinds of technical subject. It is different from the rest in this respect, that in the last resort it stands or falls by the possibility of its being communicated. The situation in most sciences is that you have your researchers and you have your popularizers. The popularizer is someone who understands what the researchers are talking about, but who can put it in ways that the rest of us can understand. But the popularizer isn't really necessary to the researchers at all. Even if he didn't exist, or if the research got so rarefied that his job became impossible, the researchers could go on happily researching as long as they could understand *each other.* Theology is not like that at all. I hope we never get to the stage in theology at which the researcher and the popularizer even become different people (though sometimes I think I see signs of it happening). But even if they do, the men on the frontiers of knowledge will be wasting their time if what they do can't be translated for the benefit of the rest of us.

Theology, after all, is only a way of talking, and God, unless the Jewish/Christian tradition which we inherit is totally wrong, cannot in the last resort be understood simply by talking. Men can only understand him by a way of living. A theology, therefore, which does not find expression or which cannot find expression in worship and service is not a theology worthy of the name. At this present time there is a tendency for theologians to drift apart from the worshipping community. Such an estrangement must in the long run vitiate the work of the theologians and impoverish the church at large. The church itself is partly to blame for this. Over the last few decades it has left the making of theology almost entirely to academics. Now I have nothing against academic theologians. Some of my best friends are academic theologians. But academics do, given the chance, tend to intellectualize things rather, and a purely intellectual theology is a contradiction in terms. The best theology has always been produced by men of the church; men who, whether they were academics or not, were *involved* with the church. The best theology has always been made by missionaries, evangelists and pastors.

Let me drop the word 'theology' for a moment. It is getting in the way rather. Let me say 'talking about God'. What's the good of my talk about God if I can't talk about him to the little girl in the primary, or to the old ladies in the Women's Bright Hour? If I have to leave my theology behind when I talk to the Sunday School or the women's meeting, it can't have been very good theology anyway.

I say this about women's meetings because when I was first ordained I took a very high and mighty attitude to such things. I was expected to put in an appearance at them, of course, and I deplored it as a stupid waste of time. I used to complain: 'This isn't what the church ordained me for, to drink tea with old ladies.' Which only goes to show what a capacity some of us have for denying the obvious. The fact staring me in the face was that this was precisely what the church did ordain me for — not to drink tea — but to proclaim the gospel to anyone who would listen. And if I couldn't put the gospel into words that meant something to old ladies in Norfolk villages it wasn't the fault

3

of the gospel and it wasn't the fault of the old ladies. Jesus wouldn't have found it impossible to talk to the Women's Bright Hour. I don't think he would have regarded it as a waste of time. And he wouldn't have talked trivialities to them either.

This is not a plea for making it easy. It is certainly not a plea for watering down what we have to say. It is a plea for thinking much harder and being much more careful about how we put things. Jesus managed to communicate. You can't convict him of superficiality or naïvety. But he didn't use much in the way of a technical vocabulary. The Word that was in the beginning, the Word that became flesh, the Word that tells us all we need to know about God, is a Word that *can* be understood, by all.

Well, that's a sort of statement of faith as to what, in my view, theology is all about, and I hope it helps to explain why I am going about things in this particular way. A famous rabbi once said: 'Do not say anything that cannot be understood at once, in the hope that it will be understood in the end.' It's not bad advice.

Well then, 'God and the future'. The proper label for this, as we all know, is 'eschatology'. Then why not use it?

If you say 'eschatology', everybody thinks, 'Ah, yes! Eschatology. We know what that means.' But they don't. They only think they do. And when you get down to it, they all mean different things. So let's start by talking about the future, which is not only a more basic idea but also a broader idea, because one of the things I want to show is that Christianity's bearing on the future brings in a lot of things that you wouldn't ordinarily class as eschatological at all.

So what is the future? It's the bit that hasn't happened yet. It's tomorrow. It's next year; next century. It's bedtime tonight. And because it hasn't happened yet we don't know, we can't be absolutely sure, what it will be like.

That's a simple enough statement for theology to start from. And in fact half of religion, *any* religion, does start precisely there. Because we don't know, for certain, what the future will be like, it fills us with hopes, with desires, with ambitions, and also with apprehensions, with worries, and with downright fears. All men somehow have to cope with the disturbing and contradictory emotions to which the uncertainty of the future gives rise. And men have always looked to religion to help them to do this.

Man is an animal, a mammal, sharing many of the instincts, urges, and certainly many of the needs, of other mammals. But he has one striking characteristic which gives him the edge over all other creatures. He can talk. Other animals *can* communicate with each other to some extent. They *can* pass on certain sorts of information. They can teach and learn from each other. But this capacity has some quite severe limitations. Broadly speaking, the animal (other than man) can only make use of experience that it has itself lived through. Man, because he can talk, can transmit *much* more of his experience to others, and learn much more from them. Experience, for him, is no longer just his own individual experience; it is the experience of his community, his people, his race, his entire species. This pooling of experience is a cumulative factor. The individual doesn't have to learn nearly everything for himself from scratch, like the cow. He can learn from others' experience, and that includes the massive store of experience of former generations.

I have a memory which extends back something like forty years. I have skills which have been building up

5

during the same period. But I have access to a 'memory' which goes back ten thousand years at least; a memory which isn't, for the most part, here in my head, but is locked away in other people's heads, as well as in books, in museums, on gramophone records and sundry other places. I can benefit, and daily do benefit, from skills which I, personally, have never acquired, but which have been building up now not for ten thousand years but for ten thousand times ten thousand. Because of this one great capacity for communication, the entire human species is able to act in some respects as if it were a single organism, an organism extending not only over the whole surface of the globe but back over the generations, a kind of humanity militant and triumphant. The advantages are, we may say, considerable.

What this amounts to is that man has an apprehension of the past and of the future which is quite denied to other species. The advantages are not only practical. Man's personality is enlarged, too. An extra dimension of *meaning* is added to his experience. 'Meaning' indeed is a function of historical awareness, awareness of how things have come to be as they are; awareness of what might happen because of what we do, and think, and are, at this moment.

These advantages have to be paid for, and they are paid for in emotion. Both awareness of the past and awareness of the future bring their problems. The past, which is the source of experience, is also the source of regret. The future, which is filled with possibilities, is filled also with fears. Man is poised between a past which he can know about but cannot alter, and a future which he can alter but cannot know about for certain.

Until quite recently man has relied heavily on religion to enable him to cope with emotions flowing from both sources, with the guilt and regret which follow him from the past, and with the hopes and apprehensions which loom out of the future.

I don't want to say a great deal about Christianity and the past, because that isn't my main theme, but I want to say a little, just to put the subject of Christianity and the future, which *is* my main theme, into perspective. One of the most important kinds of knowledge about the past is the knowledge that it might have been different. We look back into our own past and we all find things there that we wish hadn't happened. Some of them were mistakes for which we were to blame (or for which we blame ourselves, which isn't necessarily the same thing). These are things we did to ourselves. Some of them are things that were done *to* us — frightening experiences, humiliations, let-downs.

If we are to believe the psychologists, some of these old experiences lying around in our individual past are like so many unexploded bombs. If something happened to trigger them off, their charge of emotion, still unspent, could yet cause disaster. This is especially so, say the psychologists, if we have been unwise enough to convert 'I wish it hadn't happened' into 'Let's pretend it didn't happen'. The psychoanalyst sees it as his job to defuse the time bomb of the past, to render harmless dead memories and old experiences. Religion in its own way has been aiming at the same ends for a good many millennia now, and not entirely without success.

The believer is one who is as unafraid of his past as he is of his future. If we are looking for practical, concrete evidence of the difference faith makes, then I think this is one of the places where we may find it. The believer is unafraid. To begin with he is not afraid of himself. He doesn't deceive himself. Far from it! He denies nothing about his past, except its power to drag him down.

Some of us carry our failures around with us, like a

7

great burden, like the man at the beginning of *Pilgrim's Progress*. And every fresh one gets added to the pack, making it harder not to fail next time. To change the metaphor, they are like a huge debit balance on the accounts. Without it, perhaps, income and expenditure don't look *too* far apart. We *ought* to be able to manage. Or at least we'd have a fighting chance, if it weren't for that horrid red figure that gets carried forward, month after month. The believer is one whose debts are continually written off.

The Christian's acceptance of his past is not the acceptance of passivity. It is not the conviction that things could not have been otherwise, so we were not really to blame after all. It is not the pretence that the past contains nothing regrettable. It is the belief that, rightly accepted, even the regrettable things can be profitable; that through them we have learnt something (if only humility); through them grace has come to us.

The believer is one who places a particular kind of interpretation on his past — he sees it as salvation. And he does this, not by selecting from it what suits him; not by ignoring the less pleasant bits. He ignores nothing. He accepts it *all* as the way God brought him; learns from it all, but is bowed down by none of it. His past becomes not the history of failure, but the history of what God has done to him, and for him, and with him.

I shall have more to say about this in the next chapter, when we look at Israel's attitude to the past. But I say this now because it seems to me that the believer's attitude to past and future is all of a piece. They are fundamentally the same attitude — one of acceptance, openness, lack of fear.

In an earlier book which I wrote, *Living with Guilt*, I argued that one of the things that has happened in the present generation is that our guilt feelings and our

8

concern for morality have tended to re-focus themselves on corporate and communal shortcomings rather than on individual ones. We have not become less moral, and are no less obsessed with guilt than our forbears, but we tend to direct our moral attention towards social rather than personal issues. We get much more worked up, for instance, about world poverty than about sexual promiscuity. It seems to me that what has happened to our attitude to guilt, which basically springs from regret about the past, has happened also to our fears and apprehensions for the future. The most important ones are no longer individual or domestic, but communal, even cosmic.

When I was a little lad my father and mother worried about the future. They worried about whether there would be enough in the pay packet this week to cover everything (in a good week my dad was bringing in £2.15.0. before the war). They worried about whether, with unemployment in our area at some astronomical percentage, there would *be* a pay packet for much longer. They worried about what would happen if the rent went up another sixpence. Their apprehensions about the future were for the most part apprehensions about their *individual* future. They were typical enough of their generation.

Now I know there are still people in that sort of position, but they aren't typical any longer. As individuals, most of us have sufficient security not to be seriously worried about our own private future. We don't, for the most part, worry even remotely about going short of food, or about the possibility of going to the workhouse. Personal disasters of that magnitude are no longer on this side of our horizon. The individual worries we do have are far more likely to be about keeping up the repayments on the colour television or the second car. I'm not suggesting that our individual worries are trivial. They are not. Or they don't feel like it. But they are of quite a different order from those of former generations.

The characteristic apprehensions of our generation are larger scale, as it were. They seem remote, but we know that they are real. We worried a few years ago about the possibilities of nuclear war. We've put that to the back of our collective mind now, but it's still there, and it comes back into consciousness quickly enough and disturbingly enough when someone insists on testing yet another hydrogen bomb in the Pacific, and fresh pictures of those ominous and familiar mushroom clouds appear again in the papers. The fashionable worries are over-population and pollution. We know that we *could*, as a race, simply run out of resources to sustain ourselves. Or we could poison ourselves and the whole earth to death. We know that if we don't start thinking ahead *now*, we could find ourselves in intolerable difficulties in another generation or two, or perhaps less.

There are other apprehensions that seem to me to be even more important than the ones I have mentioned. They are more important in that they cause more real unease, do more real damage to our peace of mind. They are not easy to define. They are the apprehensions that spring from the very pace of change itself. You might sum them all up as the 'Where will it all end?' or the 'What will they think of next?' syndrome. Innovation and 'development' are the order of the day. We are constantly having to cope with new materials, new systems, to say nothing of new ideas. Ten years ago everything was being 'automated'. Now everything is being 'computerized'. It all amounts to the same thing, more new tricks for us poor old dogs to learn.

10

Take such a relatively simple thing as the weekly wash. Once upon a time all a woman needed in order to do the weekly wash was a bar of Sunlight soap and a minimum of expertise with a dolly stick. When mechanization reared its head it was only, at first, to provide her with a mangle or wringer, and mechanically speaking a mangle was almost the simplest machine known to science. They never went wrong, and anyone with enough sense to keep their fingers (and the baby's) out of the cogs and rollers could work them. Added to all this, of couse, you did need to know the difference between cottons and woollies, but this was the sort of distinction even a man could usually get right. Anyway, the upshot was that a lot of quite dim housewives got along perfectly well for years.

But now! I know a woman with a very expensive washing machine who for the last six months has done all her washing at the laundrette because after it broke down for the umpteenth time she decided that she couldn't afford any more repair bills. I know another whose machine *works* all right, but she still does most of the washing by hand because, to use her own words, she 'doesn't trust it'. And supposing you do trust it? And supposing your husband happens to be an electrical engineer so you're all right for repairs? Instead of sorting out into cottons and woollies you've got about forty different categories of materials; drip-dry non-iron, drip-dry minimum-iron, hand-hot wash ten-second spin, 140° wash four-minute spin, 180° wash . . . And God help the woman who gives the minimum-iron shirts the maximum-iron treatment, or the hand-hot wash nightie the 140° programme. There are complications in plenty even before we reach such joys as the petticoat which doesn't come clean at less than 180° F beautifully decorated with lace that turns yellow at 140° and all

11

sewn together with thread that *melts* at the touch of the coolest possible iron.

That was just one small example. You will be able to think of a dozen others for yourself without any effort at all. There is area after area of modern life from which we can illustrate this tendency of progress to backfire, to make things worse rather than better. There is always someone trying to sell us the new, improved something-or-other when the old, unimproved something-or-other was perfectly satisfactory. And even when the improvements are real, it is one more new thing to get used to.

And not only do we make brilliant technological breakthroughs faster than we can assimilate them or learn to live with them, we tend to concentrate our ingenuity in such odd directions. We live in a world of people who are terribly, terribly good at the spectacular but are often quite horribly inefficient at the ordinary and the mundane. If you need a transplant operation, all the resources of medical science are at your disposal. But if your child has a broken arm they'll keep him waiting in pain for four hours in the out-patient department. In a year or two we shall be able to have breakfast in London and be in San Francisco by lunch-time, but we won't be able to post a parcel from Nottingham to Leicester and get it there in less than a week. Already we can construct a vehicle of two million working parts with such reliability that it goes all the way to the moon and back with never a hitch. My last car but one, brand new, only did 7000 miles before it needed a new engine, and had two new gearboxes before it was out of guarantee. We live in such a marvellous world that you can pick up a telephone and dial your aunt in Australia, a weather forecast, the latest cricket score, a computer in Liverpool, or a recipe for supper, but you can't have your groceries delivered or

12

find a laundry that will iron your shirts. It is observations like these that prompt the question — Where will it all end?

The pace of change, even among things one thinks of as fairly permanent, is disconcerting. Anyone who lives in a big city knows that even after being away for a fortnight's holiday the skyline may be noticably different when you come back. When I visited Birmingham recently after an absence of twenty years I felt a sense of quite physical shock. I was prepared for the fact that it had changed, of course. I was not prepared for finding it totally unrecognizable.

And most of the changes no one ever *tells* us about. They just *inflict* them on us and leave us to find out. You work out that a standard 5' x 5' sheet of plywood is exactly what you need for the job in hand, and only when the job is half done do you discover that 5' x 5' sheets of plywood aren't 5' x 5' any more, but 1.5 x 1.5 metres, and you're an inch or two short. It only needs a few experiences of that sort to convince most of us that there's a conspiracy somewhere. Of course, in certain moods and certain situations change is invigorating, novelty is a challenge, but if I'm building a new cupboard on the landing I don't want to be either challenged or invigorated. I want to get the job finished as cheaply as I can. Nobody wants things to stand still, exactly, but there is so *much* change, and so much of it one can't see any sense in. We live in a world where *nothing* seems to stay the same for longer than five minutes, until some of us begin to see all change as a threat, a threat to our stability, our peace of mind. There is always something new to unsettle us, even if it's only the milk, turning up on the step one morning not in its glass bottle, but in some strange container, of some foreign material, in some alien and menacing shape.

What all this adds up to is that our apprehensions for the future are in some ways of quite a different order from those of former generations. The annoyances that 'progress' inflicts on us may seem petty. Many of them are. It is easy to make them sound amusing; though some of them are not. But in total they produce insecurity, a fear of being unable, eventually, to cope with life. We don't feel it all the time of course, but just now and again we have this slightly nightmarish feeling of living in a world which we are not entirely in control of, which we do not completely know our way around in; a world which is not altogether 'our' world. It is a feeling of vulnerability.

And to some extent it is a reasonable and justified feeling. We *are* vulnerable. For one of the effects of advanced technology is to make all of us more and more dependent on things over which we have less and less control. Our grandfathers managed perfectly well without electricity, but if the power workers go on strike and *we* have to manage without electricity life can hardly go on at all. Our grandfathers got along quite well without motor cars. But some of us, if our cars are off the road for a fortnight, wander about like lost souls, feeling as if a whole chunk of our personalities has been taken away. We're vulnerable all right.

This feeling of vulnerability, the feeling that things are going too fast for us, this 'Stop the world, I want to get off' feeling, assails everybody, I imagine, from time to time, whether they are Christians or not. But the religious man is exposed to his own peculiar form of this travel sickness. He lives not only in a world in which there are too many new things, too much of the time, but also in a world where it is becoming increasingly difficult to believe; where he is assured on all sides, even by Christian theologians if he bothers to read them, that

14

all that simplistic nonsense about God being in heaven, or about Jesus *literally* rising from the dead, or about miracles of any sort, just isn't acceptable any more. (Not only that — he is told — but of course *really* intelligent Christians never did believe it, not in that literalistic fashion.) The Christian is thus constantly tempted to see the modern world and all that belongs to it as a threat to his faith. And he is not reassured when he talks to his fellow Christians and it becomes plain to him that some, at least, of the firmest believers remain believers because there are some things about which it doesn't occur to them to think, because, fine people though they may be, they've got closed minds. The Christian thus has his own peculiar fears. He is tempted to fear for a future in which he becomes increasingly isolated, increasingly an oddity, looking more and more like a flat-earther every minute. He is tempted to fear a future in which he, too, will be forced to abandon the crutch of faith, and face the world godless.

If he is, as one might put it, *professionally* religious, he is afraid of a future in which he is going to look incredibly silly. We professionals try to protect ourselves, and our egos, of course. If we are primarily pastors we persuade ourselves that a pastor really is just a kind of social worker, and *that's* respectable enough these days. If we fancy ourselves as theologians we lightheartedly explain that religion and theology are really just ways of talking about ultimate values and that sort of thing, and God hasn't necessarily anything to do with it. Such reactions are entirely natural, for we have all been at least partly brainwashed by the world into accepting the world's estimate of ourselves, as a body of people who are trying to live in the past, who got stuck, sometime around the Middle Ages, and have been fighting rearguard actions ever since.

It is for this sort of reason that it is important to come back to that old cornerstone of the faith, the Christian hope. And Christians *are* coming back to it. In the last year or two a significant trickle of books on the subject has begun to emerge. And yet before that there was a good half-century during which the subject could scarcely be described as prominent in the church's thinking.

Why did we allow it to drop out of sight for so long? And why are we feeling the need to come back to it now? Throughout the first half of this century one very commonly heard it said, by thinking and responsible Christians, that the traditional Christian eschatological expectations were meaningless. They weren't really meaningless, though, they were just uncongenial. The Christian doctrine of the future hope was put together first by people who knew very well that their future, in worldy terms, was insecure. In the nineteenth and early twentieth centuries the feeling began to grow, and finally came to be taken for granted, that we were in control of our world and of our own destinies. The old insecurity, that men had felt as long as men had lived on this planet, was gone. The future hope of the Bible was 'meaningless'. That is to say, we didn't feel we needed it. We had hope enough in this world.

Well, that interlude is over now. We in the Western world are reverting to the natural condition of humanity, of not taking the future for granted, and the Christian hope for the future, which was designed to deal with this very insecurity, is beginning to make sense once again.

I was very impressed to read, several years ago, before the recent wave of Christian interest in the future hope had started, a book by Roger Garaudy, the French Marxist. In it Professor Garaudy was looking for a basis

16

for some kind of *rapprochement* between Marxism and the church. He was convinced that we had more in common than either of us knew. The significant thing was that what he seized on as the starting point for his proposed dialogue between Christian and Marxist was our common attitude to the future. There are significant differences, said Garaudy, between the God-centred eschatology of Christianity and the humanistic eschatology of Marxism, but the two movements are closely similar in their attitude of openness to the future. I couldn't help feeling that this very God-centredness constitutes a bigger difference than the learned professor himself appreciated, but the interesting thing, to my mind, was that a man of Garaudy's perceptiveness, who had clearly read and understood a not inconsiderable amount of Christian theology, should see eschatology as the controlling element of the faith. Not only that, but whereas the uninformed outsider would most likely say that it is in its eschatology that the church's other-worldliness most clearly shows itself, here was a very well-informed outsider arguing that it is in its eschatology that the church has its clearest points of contact with a materialistic political philosophy.

Certainly if we go back to the Bible itself we can have few doubts that the faith is concerned very largely with the future. The religion of the Old Testament is a religion of promise, if it is anything at all. (And to revert momentarily to Garaudy's thesis, it is interesting to observe that the images in which the Old Testament expresses its expectations for the future are all of them economic and political images.) The forward-looking element in the New Testament, though it tends to be differently expressed, is equally unmistakable. In both Testaments the past is important too. Faith is rooted in what *has* happened, in what God has already done. But

17

the past is there as evidence, as confirmation, as grounds for confidence in what is to come. And in both Testaments the man of faith is the man without fear; the man who is prepared to accept whatever comes — from Abraham, who went out 'not knowing . . .', to Paul, asserting that 'neither death nor life, nor angels nor principalities, nor things present nor things to come . . . will be able to separate us from the love of God'.

In one respect with regard to future expectations or future possibilities we should be able to feel particularly close to the earliest Christians, and this is a respect which I have already touched on. For most of the history of Western Christianity it has been the future expectations of the individual which have received most attention. His eternal fate, his eternal reward, or his eternal judgment and condemnation were expressed in terms of personal immortality, of heaven or hell for his individual soul. The idea of cosmic judgment was never lost, but it did recede into the background.

Now for the earliest Christians it was the cosmic aspect of the future expectation which was primary. The judgment, for them, was not so much a question of heaven and a new earth. It was God reconciling the stars falling from the sky. It was the making of a new heaven and a new earth. It as God reconciling the cosmos to himself. That is to say, they regarded the total destruction of the world as they knew it as a daily possibility, and this dominated their expectations for the future.

So we have this in common with them, for we, too, realistically face the possibility of the end of the world as we know it. We could, by design or error, blow the whole thing up in a manner that would be awful to contemplate but would at least make a satisfying bang, though we are more likely, on present form, to opt for the more disgusting method of poisoning ourselves and the earth slowly to death. And here, of course, we put our finger on a difference, or apparent difference, between the earliest Christians' expectations and our own. They anticipated a destruction which would be brought about directly by God or the agents of God, or by the supernatural powers of darkness with his permission and consent. We envisage an end which would be self-inflicted, an act of human self-destruction compounded of human wickedness and human folly.

I am not sure that, theologically speaking, these two ways of presenting the matter are quite as far apart as they look. Nevertheless, there *are* significant differences between them and certain important differences of attitude do follow from them. Twentieth-century Christians, contemplating the possible end of the world, or the end of civilization as they know it, would certainly be inclined to interpret it as a divine judgment, which unbelievers would not. But in one important respect most twentieth-century Christians would share the unbelievers' assumptions. Most twentieth-century men, believers and unbelievers alike, contemplate the end of the world as they know it *as the worst thing that could possibly happen*. The earliest Christians did not share this assumption. On the contrary, they looked forward to the end of the world with the greatest eagerness, and they hardly ever opened their mouths in prayer without including a request that it should happen soon.

This was not because they had any complacent expectations about what it would be like. The imagery which they use to describe it is very varied, but what they are trying to say by means of that imagery adds up to a fairly consistent picture. They are entirely consistent in their assertions that the end and the events

19

that lead up to it will be unspeakably horrifying. They are consistent in their expectations that it will be unspeakably horrifying not only for the wicked, but for the righteous too. Indeed, they often suggest that at least in the early stages it will actually be worse for the righteous. But they are also consistent in their anticipation that for the righteous the terror, the suffering and the tortures will be *just* bearable, and consistent above all in their conviction that beyond the terror there will be peace, and that beyond the end of the world as they know it there will be another world, new-created, good.

At the very point, therefore, at which our expectations for the future come closest to those of the earliest Christians, our attitudes most sharply differ. We shall not have understood the future hope of Jesus and the apostles until we can contemplate the possibility of the end of the world as we know it, and do so without regret.

2

Attitudes to the Future found in the Old Testament

When I was a little boy, a *very* little boy, I used to stay quite often with my grandfather and grandmother, and I have very clear memories of their house even now. And one of my clearest memories is of the bedroom which I used to sleep in when I stayed there, with its brass bedstead so high off the floor that a small boy had literally to *climb* into bed, and its patchwork quilt. I can recall the distinctive feel and smell of that patchwork quilt now. But the thing I remember best was the two pictures on the wall, a pair. They were of Moses and Abraham; Abraham just about to leave Ur of the Chaldees, and Moses on the summit of Mount Nebo, overlooking the Promised Land. If I could see them again now I have no doubt that I should consider them artistically wanting, but they impressed me greatly at the time. And they must indeed in a sense have been good pictures, because what I remember about them was something that I'm sure the artist was most concerned to convey. I remember the eyes. Both Abraham and Moses were looking into the distance. Nine-tenths of what the Old Testament has to say to mankind was in that look. It was the look of men who

21

are living for the future.

Let us examine that phrase for a minute, because it has some beautiful ambiguities in it which illustrate both what the hope of biblical man is and what it is not. What is it to 'live for the future'?

I can remember times when I have lived for the future; the last year before I got married, for instance, when I and my fiancée were living a hundred miles apart. I lived for the future, crossing off the days on my calendar. It wasn't a pleasant feeling. I remember doing a clerking job for about eighteen months while I went through the long process of getting accepted as a Methodist ordinand. I had to sit all day adding up figures. And I'm the sort of chap whose idea of hell is to be faced with an account book. I lived for the future. I lived for the weekends when I could go rock climbing; for next year, when, as I hoped, I would go to college.

This kind of 'living for the future' is a painful experience because it turns the present into nothing more than an interlude, something to be lived through, a barrier between us and the desired goal. So we spend our lives 'wishing our time away'.

There is another kind of 'living for the future' which is deceptive. I hope I can explain what I mean. I have certainly met examples of it. You meet a man, now and again, who, although he spends most of his waking hours in the sacred calling of making money, really knows, inside him, that this isn't what life is all about. So he promises himself something better, later. When he retires, he tells himself, he'll buy a lot of records and seriously start listening to music. Or, when he retires he'll really take up fishing properly. Or, when he retires he'll buy a bungalow in the country with a really big garden and spend his time gardening (very satisfying, gardening).

Plans of this sort rarely come to anything. What such a man almost inevitably finds is that retirement isn't a magic formula that changes the habits of a lifetime. Unless he has done something, much, much earlier than that, to cultivate the interests he has set his heart on, to develop the skills, the expertise, the attitudes of mind, the capacities for appreciation which his interest demands, then he will discover that gardening all day is terribly tedious; that he can't concentrate on music for more than twenty minutes; that his interest in fishing has evaporated after the first three hours.

What such a man has done is to live for a future which has no organic connexion with the present. He has put present and future into watertight compartments, different worlds, almost. The present is what he uses to earn the money to pay for the future. He is, in effect, buying the future at the cost of the present. This isn't very pleasant either, and anyway it doesn't usually work.

There is a kind of hope for the future which writes off the past. This is the future hope of the technocrats which is always writing off last year's model. This is the future hope of too much of the modern world, which writes off old buildings, old inventions, old insights, old values, as irrelevant, irrelevant for no better reason than that they are old.

But the kind of living for the future which Moses and Abraham do is of a different sort. Their future hope is of a different sort. It is not a future hope which deprives the present of its meaning, which turns it into an unpleasant interim, something to be lived through. It is a future hope which *makes sense of* the present. Abraham and Moses have got that look in their eye because what they are doing now makes sense in the light of what is to come, and what is to come makes

23

sense in the light of what they are doing now. And what is more, the things they are doing now and the things they hope for in the future have some solid justification in their experiences of the past. Abraham receives no more of the land than is sufficient for him to bury his dead. But it is a kind of token that the land will be his. Moses has gone to all that trouble leading a mob of his ungrateful fellow-countrymen to the edge of a promised land in which he himself will never tread. But he looks forward, he takes possession of it with his eyes.

Abraham and Moses have that look about them because they know that past, present and future; where they stand now, where they stood forty years ago, and where their children will stand after them, is the realm of grace. In this kind of 'living for the future' past, present and future are cemented together, each giving meaning to and taking its meaning from the others.

This kind of 'living for the future' turns the present into something which is not *just* a step on the way to something better, but which is at the same time an achievement in its own right. Does that sound like a contradiction? Moses would have understood. I remember the look in his eyes as he stood on Nebo, and I know that he would have understood how it is that achievement and promise, fulfilment and expectation, can be one and the same.

Let me now, as I did in the last chapter, look briefly at the question of attitudes to the past, because only so can we see how the Old Testament view, its idea of religion as promise, hangs together.

We often talk of our 'experience' of the past as if this was something that just happened to us; as if we were the passive receivers, or sufferers, of what time and chance chose to do to us. In our more careful moments we know that this is not so. 'Experience' has two

24

components: there is what happens; and there is what you let it do to you, what you make of it.

I once heard two people discussing their holidays. One had had such foul weather that the holiday had been a total washout. The other said, well, the weather was a bit mixed but it certainly hadn't been intolerable, and in the event they had had a thoroughly good time.

Later in the conversation it emerged that they had both been at the same seaside resort — for the same fortnight.

What they had said about the weather had said less about meteorological facts than about the holidaymakers themselves, about their characters, attitudes of mind. In spite of having been in the same place at the same time, their *experience* had been quite different.

The early rabbis, for whom I have a great respect, said something rather similar, in their picturesque way. They insisted that when God gave the commandments on Mount Sinai Moses was not the only man there (as a merely superficial reading of scripture might suggest). Every nation of the world had a representative on Sinai on that occasion. And God gave the commandments not only in Hebrew but in every language known. It was just that the others didn't listen. This isn't only a neat reply to the objection that God's choice of Israel implies divine favouritism (though I think that was the main motive for inventing the story). It also implies that when Israel interpreted the things that happened to her as evidence of divine interest and guidance, it wasn't necessarily because the things that happened to her were all that different from the things that happened to everybody else. It was because she was blessed with that kind of interpreters.

Long before the rabbis started inventing their fables Amos had seen the same point. He puts into God's mouth the question, 'Did I not bring up the Philistines from the Caphtor and the Syrians from Kir?' (9.7). He is suggesting that Israel's history is not really unique. How many other nations' ancestors escaped from slavery across mud flats and had the good luck to find the tide in their favour? How many had comparable experiences? What miracles attended the Philistines' exodus from Caphtor? What pillar of cloud and fire led the Syrians from Kir? True, we don't find the Philistines or Syrians elaborating a covenant theology or celebrating the might acts of God in history. But is it because their past was all that different from Israel's? Or shall we find, when the truth at last comes out, that they too spent the same fortnight at Bognor?

Israel's history is salvation history because she claims the past as the realm of grace. I said earlier, speaking of the individual believer, that for him the past, in so far as it involves guilt, is really dead. It doesn't hamper him any more. But that doesn't mean that it is forgotten. The lessons of the past are still there, before him, and *must not be* forgotten. In this sense the past is not dead at all but is very much alive. It is certainly alive for Israel. She must keep harking back to it, bringing up again and again her great experiences; re-living them; celebrating them; sucking the juice out of them over and over. The individual Israelite is told to recall them and to talk about them, when he goes to bed and when he gets up; when he sits at home and when he goes to work. He is to write them on his doorpost so that he remembers them every time he goes in or out. He is to recount them to his children, reminding them that a wandering Aramaean was their father; that they were slaves in Egypt; that the Lord their God with a strong hand and an outstretched arm delivered them.

But it isn't just the highlights of her past that Israel

claims. It certainly isn't just the pleasant bits, the bits that do her credit. Her people remember, and recite with loving care, the names of the staging places in the wilderness wanderings – the whole list! What possible usefulness could there be in that? They didn't even know any longer where half of these places *were*. But every staging place matters, every milepost, every inch of the way, because it is the way God brought us.

There are two significant things to notice about this list of staging places. Where it crops up in later Jewish literature we find a neat piece of re-interpretation happening. The list ends '. . . and from Mattanah to Naheniel, and from Nahaliel to Bamoth'. And for the later interpreters the *meaning* of these names has become far more important then their location. For Mattanah means 'gift', Nahaliel means 'the inheritance of God', and Bamoth means 'high places'. This, they explain, is the end of the way God leads, from Gift to Inheritance, and from Inheritance to the Heights. By this stage in the tradition therefore these are not just places, but promises.

The second feature of the list is more important. It includes the places of failure. And there were plenty of those, for there are very few parts of the history of salvation which reflect credit on the people who recounted it. But at every place, of trials, battles, grumblings, even outright rebellion, Israel felt that she had met God. At every site she could say, 'Here, too, the Lord helped us: *and* here, *and* here, *and* here.'

The Old Testament writers, therefore, without romanticizing Israel's past at all, claim all of it as a kind of journey during which God has been with them. And they look forward with confidence because they see the future with exactly the same eyes. This forward-lookingness, this emphasis on promise, seems to have been characteristic of the faith of Israel as far back as we can trace it. It appears to be there in traditions which emanate from a time before there *was* an Israel. These traditions originated (unless our whole understanding of the Old Testament is seriously at fault) among nomads, and the nomad is one whose whole life is spent travelling hopefully; whose every arrival is but a stage on the way to a better country.

But those early Israelites reached their promised land. They settled down and they began to live in cities. At this point Israel might have been forgiven if she had dropped the note of expectation and considered herself to have arrived. Some, perhaps many, of her people were apparently tempted to do exactly that, to settle down not only physically but spiritually too. Her leaders (though it was a struggle) allowed her to do no such thing. They went on, as it were, to seek a better city.

What happened was that the *form* of the hope changed, or the form in which it was expressed changed, but the *fact* of hope remained. The hope became, you might say, urbanized. It also came to be closely bound up with national aspirations, with the desire for independence, or, when they *had* independence, for empire. The hope tended to centre upon the Lord's anointed, the king, and upon the holy city, with its sanctuary, where God's presence was, guaranteeing Israel's security, and where at the great festivals God could meet his people and assure them of his favour.

By the end of the reign of David Israel seemed to have achieved most of what she was hoping for. She had an anointed, of great wisdom and virtue; she had a royal city and a royal sanctuary where the ark, sign of God's presence, was enshrined. She had attained something very like empire. And this is where her characteristic

28

way of looking at things is most in evidence: having attained all this, she regarded it as a step on the way to something better. She saw it as a token of what was still to come.

Throughout the period of the kingdoms the prophets saw it as their job to deepen and refine the hope of Israel. They don't say to her, 'It's wrong to hope'. They assume that it is right; that God always has better things in store. What they insist on is that there is nothing automatic about the hope's fulfilment.

Now there is a vast amount I could say about this very important issue, the prophetic note of judgment and what it contributes to the future perspective of Israelite religion, but I am leaving it out because there are other things which for our present purposes I am more concerned to draw out.

I want first of all to draw attention to the imagery the prophets use. I am doing no more than draw attention to it, partly because I am sure that most readers will be familiar enough with it already; partly, again, for the sake of spending more time on other things. But the imagery is important because it keeps on cropping up, in one form or another, all the way from Amos and the psalmists through to the apocalyptists, the New Testament, and on from the New Testament down as far as Charles Wesley, Sankey and Moody, and on beyond.

Perhaps I oughtn't to call it 'imagery', because this really begs the question about how literally they took it. Let me just call it 'the language in which the future hope is talked about'. There is first of all the political language. The future is envisaged in terms of the reign of a righteous king. The Israelites exhibited their perennial human optimism, like the rest of us, in their belief that the next government would be better than the one they'd got. Bound up with the political language there is the military language. The Lord's anointed was destined to win a resounding victory over the Lord's (and his people's) enemies. This was how the new age would dawn. And right through the apocalyptic writers (like the author of Daniel, for example) and beyond them the new age is still seen as being inaugurated by a battle, even when that battle has been transmuted from an earthly war into a war between the hosts of heaven and the hosts of the powers of darkness.

And then, rather incongruously at first sight, there is the language of agriculture, of harvest. It isn't really incongruous. In order to enter the new age of peace and prosperity it isn't only necessary to win wars. It is also necessary to get the economy right, to raise productivity, to improve the balance of trade, and so on. And in the conditions in which all ancient societies operated 'the economy' meant agriculture. A people with an agrarian economy is bound to frame its expectations for a better tomorrow in terms of bumper harvests. When Jesus looked at the fields 'white unto harvest' and saw them as a sign that the new age was about to dawn, this wasn't just a metaphor which he had thought up off the cuff. People in Palestine had been using that kind of language for at least a thousand years, and maybe more.

But the language of harvest and the language of war were also brought together in Israel's mind by another odd circumstance. Autumn, just after the grape harvest, is the one slack time in the Palestinian agricultural year. The last harvest is in, but next year's ploughing can't start (we are talking of the days before tractors) until the autumn rains soften the ground enough. For this reason, in ancient times this period was the season for war. It was this that brought together in the annual cycle of events the celebrations of victory (if there were any victories to be had) and of harvest. The fruits of the earth and the fruits of war fell due more or less together in the Palestinian economy. This is why these two apparently disparate elements intermingle in so much of the Bible's literature of hope.

'They rejoice before thee as with joy at the harvest, as men rejoice when they divide the spoil ... For to us a child is born, to us a son is given' (Isa. 9.2-7). The combination of images (harvest, war, kingship) is characteristic. In Isaiah 63 the same combination appears, and this harvest is explicitly the grape harvest, the vintage. The images, indeed, are completely fused. When the Lord comes, with his 'apparel red' and his 'garments like his that treads in the winepress', it is because he has 'trodden the winepress alone'; which is to say, that he 'trod down the peoples in (his) anger ... and poured out their lifeblood on the earth'. Vintager and bloody conqueror are one and the same. The book of Joel makes the same combination but stands the images on their heads. Instead of being conceived in terms of rich harvests and of victory, the day of the Lord is envisaged as both defeat and dearth. The poetry passes, often imperceptibly, from one image to the other, so that at some points the reader simply doesn't know whether what is being described is the ravaging, destroying army of the enemy, or the ravaging, destroying locusts eating up the land.

The image, or the expectation, of the bumper harvest passes over into another, the image of the restoration of paradise. In the good time coming 'the ploughman will overtake the reaper' (Amos 9.13). The harvests will be so big that there will be no time to gather them before the next is due to be sown. In those days 'even the desert shall rejoice and blossom' (Isa. 35.1). In this kind of imagery it isn't just a matter of ordinary good harvests; an element of what we should call the miraculous has crept in. When we get on beyond the Old Testament, to the literature of the inter-testamental period, this 'miraculous' element in the descriptions of the new age takes over completely. For in the new age every vine will bear a thousand clusters, and every cluster have a thousand grapes, and every grape will yield ten barrels of wine. (Throughout the Bible an abundance of wine is always a feature of God's kingdom.)

Now when we look closely at this imagery, or this language in which the future hope is expressed, we find a very definite development in it. The way the images are used changes perceptibly and significantly between one period and another. The way the pre-exilic prophets use their imagery makes it pretty clear that though they looked forward to a better time, they saw it as being connected with the present state of affairs by the normal historical processes of cause and effect, by processes that we all understand and that we can read about in the newspapers. If Israel was to gain independence and empire it would be through the ordinary processes of economic recovery and military victory; because at long last she would get her balance of payments right, get the economy moving; because she would then be able to mount a serious war effort; because her generals would be cleverer and her troops braver than the enemy's. If there was to be a righteous king it would be because the house of David, the existing ruling house, would throw up a prince whose character would be strong enough, whose education careful enough, whose advisers wise enough, to make him into a second David, and a better David.

I do not think anyone is seriously suggesting nowadays that the pre-exilic prophets, or anyone in the pre-exilic period, thought about the future in any other than these rather down-to-earth terms. They idealize the future to some extent, no doubt, but the way they envisage it is essentially naturalistic. There is nothing, as we should see it, 'supernatural' about the way it would happen. (The texts quoted above from the books of Amos and Isaiah were not spoken by those prophets themselves, or during their time.)

What happens at the time of the exile is that there is a change, as it seems to me, not at first in the way the future is conceived, but in the way it is talked about. I cannot here make out my case in detail, for that would involve lengthy quotation from the sources, but it seems to me that the prophets at the time of the exile (I am thinking here mainly of the one we call Deutero-Isaiah, who was responsible for Isaiah chapters 40-55, but also to a lesser extent of Ezekiel), though they go on using the same images, the same *sort* of language to describe the future, begin to use it in a different manner.

I still don't think that Deutero-Isaiah is seriously anticipating anything that we should call a miracle. I don't think he *literally* expects the wilderness to break out into singing as Israel marches across it, or the desert to burst into bloom. But the way he uses words leaves them open to that misunderstanding. He is describing what he hopes and trusts is going to happen, the rescue of his people from foreign captivity and foreign domination, and he is trying to bring out what he sees as the significance of these events by describing them in very highly coloured and imaginative poetic language. We know that he *is* given to the use of very picturesque language, and we can sometimes check that he is using it quite consciously as metaphor and doesn't mean it to be taken literally. He can make free use of pagan mythology, for example, and talk about God creating the

33

world by cutting Rahab the chaos-monster in pieces, by piercing the sea-dragon. And we know he didn't literally believe *that*: his own ideas about creation are much more sophisticated. Deutero-Isaiah didn't believe in Rahab the chaos-monster any more than John Milton believed in all those classical deities that he kept on dragging into his poems. We can thus check that Deutero-Isaiah is the sort of writer who makes quite conscious use of metaphor, and sometimes of quite extravagant metaphor. A similar case can be made out for Ezekiel.

Now much of the picturesque language which Deutero-Isaiah and Ezekiel use is of a kind that can broadly be called 'eschatological'. This doesn't mean that it always implies an end of the world, though occasionally you could read that into it. It is eschatological in the sense that it seems to suggest that the bad times are suddenly going to turn into good times, and that the good times are going to come about, not because of the effects of normal political and economic factors, but because God has decided that they should, and because he, personally, as it were, has taken a hand in rather spectacular fashion.

Now again, I think we can see that the prophets who use such language don't really intend it to be taken in this way. Deutero-Isaiah, when you get down to it, has got just as shrewd an idea as any other prophet of the political machinery by which he expects his predictions to be fulfilled. He is pinning much of his expectations on Cyrus and his anticipated military conquests, and on Cyrus's known liberal policies towards subject peoples. His eschatological language is not meant to be taken literally; it is used in order to show just how earth-shatteringly significant he sees these coming events to be. For this reason he can even talk as if they will be the

34

end of the world, the end of the cosmic order.

In that last paragraph, without premeditation, I found I had resorted to the phrase 'earth-shatteringly significant'. When anybody uses a phrase like that we don't dream of taking it literally. However significant the thing referred to may be, we don't actually expect the world to start coming apart at the seams. Deutero-Isaiah, I am convinced, is using words in the same sort of way. In fact, when we analyse his language, we find that he resorts quite impartially both to imagery that talks in terms of the end of the world and imagery that talks in terms of its beginning, to protology (if you like) as readily as to eschatology. But whether he says, 'What God is about to do is like the end of the world', or 'What God is about to do is like the creation all over again', he is making exactly the same point. It is just that in the latter case nobody dreams of taking his language as other than poetic imagery, whereas in the former they have sometimes imagined that he meant quite literally what he said.

The exilic prophets, like their predecessors, believed that God was running the world, and that he had got history under control. Both they and their predecessors agreed that the machinery by which he exercized his control was mostly the well-understood machinery of political and economic life. The 'radicalizing' language of the exilic prophets is not meant to suggest that God was resorting to new methods, short-circuiting the familiar processes, winding things up or creating new systems, *but it did leave itself open to being understood in that way.* It was probably first understood in that way quite shortly after the exilic prophets' own time.

Trito-Isaiah, the man or the group of men responsible for Isaiah chapters 56-66, uses much the same sort of language, on the surface, as Deutero-Isaiah, but I fancy that a difference has already crept in. I have a strong feeling (though I want to do a little more research into this) that at least sometimes when Trito-Isaiah uses talk about the end of the world he really means it; means it in a way his predecessor never did.

But whether this is true of Trito-Isaiah or not it is certainly true of the apocalyptists. Probably the earliest of the true apocalyptists was the writer of Daniel. He set a fashion which produced a spate of apocalyptic writings in the period between the Testaments. They have titles like The Similitudes of Enoch or The Assumption of Moses. They are mostly ascribed to ancient worthies and purport to be accounts of visions which their alleged authors had. They seem to spend quite a lot of their time talking about the end of the world, and this is usually seized on as one of their outstanding features. I'm not sure, though, that it is the most significant thing about them. Between the later prophets and the early apocalyptists the difference in future perspective doesn't seem to me to be all that great. They are both interested in the future, but it is nearly always the *immediate* future. The apocalyptists tend to disguise this by their technique of ascribing everything to ancient authors, but the far future which the alleged ancient author is talking about is the real author's immediate future. So if the author of Daniel, for instance, seems to talk quite a lot about the end of the world, the real reason for his interest is that he thinks the end is going to be next week. Daniel, like the prophets, is still interested in the future mainly because of the effects it has on the present. The real originality of the apocalyptists lies in the way they think the present and the future are connected together. The prophets thought that the future would emerge by the well-understood processes of cause and effect. History

36

for them was still a continuous process. For the apocalyptists there is a break somewhere in the sequence. They have lost faith in politics. No future worth having, they think, can emerge from the normal processes of history. Something different has to happen. God can do no more with the present system or within the present system. He must shatter it and start again. What they have done is to take the 'radicalizing' language of people like Deutero-Isaiah and literalize it. They have taken Deutero-Isaiah's 'It will be like a miracle', and they have said, 'It will be a miracle'. They have invented, in the process, the *Deux ex machina*, the God who comes on stage at the end to sort things out and to clear up the mess.

If we confine our attention to the book of Daniel, we find that whatever sort of wedge may have been driven between the present and the future as far as *causality* is concerned, *psychologically* the two still hang together. The focus of interest is still 'now in the time of this mortal life'. It is the implications of the future for present existence that are uppermost in mind.

'Daniel's' readers are faced with an all too real crisis; with persecution, with torture, with death. These are the conditions which have always stimulated interest in the future hope. Daniel, as I have said, takes a view characteristic of the apocalyptic writers when he demonstrates his complete loss of faith in the normal processes of history. If salvation is coming, it is not because anyone in his right mind would predict its coming through ordinary political means. Militarily Israel hasn't a chance. Anyone who dares to hope in such a time is hoping in the teeth of the evidence. Yet salvation will come, says Daniel. History will work to its predetermined end, but not because of anything that men do about it. The future is determined not by the policies of governments or by human decisions of any sort, but by God's iron laws. Things happen not by what *we* understand as cause and effect, but because it is so decreed, because there is a destiny which shapes our ends, rough hew them how we will.

In spite of all this Daniel's future hope is as far as could be from 'pie in the sky'. He can be quite terrifyingly realistic. He has to be. When people are in the kind of mess Daniel's readers were in (and you can read the books of Maccabees to find out what sort of a mess it was), you may try to cheer them up, but you mustn't, in the name of common humanity, fool them with false or shallow promises. The realism comes out in the story of Shadrach, Meshach and Abed-nego (Dan. 3.17). They are faced with a demand that was all too familiar to many of Daniel's readers at the time, either to renounce their religious principles or be put to a horrible death. When threatened by the king the three reply: 'Our God, whom we serve, is able to deliver us from the burning fiery furnace, and out of your hand, O king.' That's faith. But they go on, and this is where the realism of faith comes in: '*But if not*, be it known unto you, O king, we will not serve your gods . . .'

This is the sort of extremity which shows what the future hope is all about. The future hope is about the way I face the crisis in front of me *now*. Those of Daniel's readers who in real life had to face burning fiery furnaces knew that '*if not*' were the operative words. What Shadrach and the rest are saying is 'We have a hope for the future. Yes! We have faith in God. Yes! We don't go back for an instant on those beliefs. Nevertheless, *even if we are wrong* . . . . Damn you, Nebuchadnezzar.' There is a tremendous moral here for the twentieth-century believer, or half-believer. There *is* a sort of faith which doesn't conceive how it can be wrong. But it's a sort that isn't even an option for most of us these days. There is another sort, and it may not be a worse sort either, which thinks that it very easily might be — a faith which is a kind of act of defiance.

Later apocalypticism loses, it seems to me, the sense of realism. I think it loses not only the causal connexion between the present and the future but the psychological connexion too. For Daniel the future hope is still what gives the present meaning. I think that in later apocalyptic the future hope devalues the present. It turns the present into an interlude to be lived through, a period of waiting, of sitting around until God should choose to act. It becomes interested in the end of the world, not because the end of the world is next week so we must remember to stop the milk, but for its own sake. With these later apocalyptists we see the emergence of a real, literal eschatology, and it looks to me like the great betrayal. Daniel, whatever changes have taken place in his conception of history and of the way the process works, is still, at the point where it matters most, on the same side as the prophets, which is the same side as Abraham and Moses. These people, the later apocalyptists, no longer are. They are not without their virtues. They do grasp the fact that the future hope involves not only the believer but the creation. They also grasp the very important fact that hope for the future does not lie in human institutions or in human nature. But they have drawn the wrong conclusions from this valid insight. They have taken Daniel's determinism and made it fatalism. For them the future hope is no longer about the crisis in front of me now, it *is* pie in the sky.

It is worth noting that there is very little of this kind of apocalyptic in the Old and New Testaments. Most of it is in the inter-testamental and apocryphal literature,

39

and there was a lot of it in the air at the time when Jesus taught and the gospels were written. This kind of literal eschatology has left its mark on the Bible, but it does not represent the main thrust of the Bible's ideas of the future hope. If modern man looks on this sort of eschatology as irrelevant; if modern Christian preachers have stopped preaching it, it is because they are led by a sure instinct. It has very little indeed to say to us.

3

The Nature of Christian Hope and the Possibilities of the Holy Spirit

The last chapter took us, with one or two meanderings, through some Old Testament attitudes to the future, finishing with the developed eschatological thinking of the later apocalyptic writers. The Jews of New Testament times took much of this apocalyptic thinking for granted. Apocalyptic imagery and language was part of the furniture of their minds. It might seem natural for us to go on, therefore, and see how the New Testament writers used and developed these apocalyptic notions. I think, however, that to do this carries the risk of distorting what the New Testament has to say.

Rather than jump in at the deep end of New Testament eschatology, therefore, I want us to go back, and to remind ourselves of where we started. We started by talking about the future; about the apprehensions that arise out of the future; and about what faith has to say about them. How does the New Testament deal with these apprehensions? What attitude or attitudes to the future does it encourage. What kind of hopes for the future does it stimulate? If we ask these broader questions I think we shall come round eventually to what is more narrowly called 'New Testament eschatology' and see it in better perspective, as part of a larger whole.

The Palestinian peasant of biblical times had some pretty concrete reasons for worrying about the future. His livelihood depended on what he could grow on a small plot of land. And much of the land which the Palestinian peasant cultivates so carefully is the sort of stony, hill ground that in this country we should consider only two possible uses for, grazing sheep or planting trees. If the harvest in any year was poor he rarely had much to fall back on. His concern for the future was engaged with questions like: where am I going to get corn to feed my family until the next harvest? How am I going to raise the interest due on the loan for last year's seed? If they foreclose the mortgage on the house, where are we going to live? If I can't get the blankets out of pawn before the winter, how shall we keep warm?

Jesus, who was himself a Palestinian peasant, doesn't give any glib answers. His advice, briefly, is 'Concentrate on today's problems, and leave tomorrow's until tomorrow.' All the instincts of modern Western man rebel against this advice. Most of us have an obsession with security, though I think this is perhaps less common among the young. Certainly Jesus's advice is of a kind that is easily misrepresented and misunderstood. I am not going into the difficulties and details of it now, but wish only to indicate rather broadly what his attitude is. The effect of his advice is to counsel complete openness to the future. What the future will bring needn't be worried about. Do the job in front of you; the job God is giving you to do, now. And when you get hungry, not before, you can start bothering about the next meal.

An analysis of the Lord's Prayer is interesting in this

connection, because most of its petitions are concerned with the future, as I suppose most prayer naturally is.

Thy kingdom come: All I need say about this from our present point of view is that the prayer for the coming of God's kingdom is effectively a prayer for the total abandonment of the world to divine control. The expansion, 'thy will be done . . .', makes this clear.

Give us this day . . .: This is the most vital petition for our purposes. It seems to be in line with the accepted rabbinic doctrine that one day's bread is all that one is entitled to ask for. To ask for more than one day's food at a time is faithlessness, and to ask for anything fancier than bread is greed.

Forgive us our trespasses: This is the only petition of the Lord's Prayer which concerns itself with the past.

But now we come to a second important aspect of prayer about the future: *And lead us not into temptation.* This is very much an eschatological petition. It is not really 'temptation' in our everyday sense of the word that the prayer has in mind. A better translation would be 'trial' or 'testing'. It has quite a technical sense. Any first century Jew or Christian, familiar as he was with the language and ideas of apocalyptic, would understand this as a reference to the great horrors that the apocalyptists anticipated would precede the coming of the kingdom. It is asking to be spared these horrors – or is it? If we take into account what the New Testament says elsewhere about these birth pangs of the new age, perhaps the prayer has a rather more restricted purpose. Elsewhere it seems to be assumed that the Lord must not be expected to spare his people the agonies of the last time, but that he might be prevailed on to spare them the very worst, to cut it short a little (Mark 13.20).

Mark 13.14ff. hints rather fearsomely at some of the

things that the faithful can expect before they see God's kingdom finally established. They are hints that would strike at the very bowels of people as familiar as the Palestinians were with riot and civil disturbance, with the antics of self-appointed freedom fighters and urban guerillas, and with the reprisals that followed them from the security forces of the occupying power. And in the middle of the description Jesus says, 'Pray!'

Pray what? What would *you* pray? What would any of us pray in the face of such possibilities? You would pray, and so would I, that it might not happen, that violence and this constant assault on every decent human feeling might be averted, done away with.

Jesus says, 'Pray — that it may not happen in winter.' My God! Couldn't he think of a better prayer than that? But Jesus constantly staggers us, not only by the things he dares to pray for, but by the things he doesn't.

Jesus is here standing on the same ground as Amos and Jeremiah before him. He assumes that there is a point beyond which one ought not to pray for the just judgment of God to be averted. Once human sin has gone so far as to make judgment inevitable and repentance unthinkable the most one ought to ask is for the edge to be taken off the pain. 'Pray, that it may not happen in the winter.'

Mark 13, to which we have been referring, is a composite and complex chapter, variations on the theme of the gruesomeness of the future. Some portions seem to be dealing with the fall of Jerusalem to the Romans; some with the anticipated persecution of Jesus's followers; some, quite possibly, with genuine eschatology, the end of the world and the last judgment. But the whole chapter bears witness to the Christian conviction that the statement, 'The future is in the hands of God', must *not* be taken to mean, 'We're all

44

going to have a lovely time.' Openness to the future means, for the Christian, openness to suffering, and even, openness to the possibility of death.

For the future contains, for the Christian, not only salvation but judgment. And the faith of the Christian goes even beyond the 'if not . . .' of Shadrach, Meshach and Abed-nego, because he knows that when God judges his world it will be his job to accept willingly his share, and more than his share, of the world's suffering; because he, out of all the sufferers, will have hope. The Christian must suffer and hope, because suffering is his job, and hope is his job. And he must go on suffering and hoping, though the twelve legions of angels do not materialize and there is no fourth man in the fire.

This openness to suffering, and even death, is one of the themes that ties the various parts of the New Testament most firmly together. It is found not only in the gospels but in Acts and in the epistles; it is found among the martyrs of the early centuries. It marks the early boldness of Peter and John, with their reasoned defiance of high priestly authority (Acts 4.13-20). It is characteristic of Paul, 'afflicted in every way, but not crushed; perplexed, but not driven to despair; persecuted, but not forsaken; struck down, but not destroyed' (II Cor. 4.8f.); Paul asserting that 'neither death nor life, nor angels nor principalities, nor things present nor things to come, nor powers, nor height, nor depth, nor anything else in all creation' can separate him from the love of God which is in Christ Jesus his Lord; Paul again, claiming that 'whether we live or whether we die, we are the Lord's'; for whom, at the last, to live is Christ, but to die and be with Christ is better still. The same theme links the readers to whom 1 Peter is addressed, expecting their 'fiery trials', with Jesus himself, setting his face steadfastly towards Jerusalem;

the same Jesus who, for the joy that was set before him, 'endured the cross, despising the shame'.

This is one of the things that openness to the future means in the New Testament. It isn't just a matter of not worrying about the electricity bill. It is a matter of claiming the future, whatever it brings, as we claim the past, whatever it has brought, as the realm of grace. It is a matter of asserting that the world of the future, like the world of the past, will be a world where God meets us; of claiming all experience, before it happens, as experience of God, and every river we shall ever cross as Jordan.

But there is another aspect of openness to the future, as the New Testament writers understand it. To introduce it let me, for a moment, examine the word 'hope'. 'Hope' is a good New Testament word. St Paul even describes his God as 'the God of hope' (Rom. 15.13).

But at first sight, to my mind at any rate, 'hope' isn't a very good word to use in theology — or at least not as it is normally understood in English. Perhaps the Greek word that the New Testament uses had a slightly different flavour, but in English the word 'hope' lacks the element of confidence. The man who puts 25p on the treble chance every week does it in hope. But unless he's a fool he doesn't actually do it with confidence. The 'hope' that the man doing his pools feels is something far, far removed from what the Christian feels when he contemplates what God has in store for him.

Let us consider a better parallel. The child looks forward to Christmas. In hope? Yes, it *is* hope, the word is appropriate. But the context gives it a peculiar and distinctive flavour. He hopes he'll get roller skates. Confidently? Yes and no. It may not *be* roller skates. But even if it isn't, he knows that mum and dad will

46

make sure it's something he really wants, something exciting. Mum and dad *are* capable of surprising him (in a nice way, of course). They're capable of cooking up something he doesn't expect; something so marvellous that he didn't even dream of asking for it. They might even have thought of something marvellous that he's never even heard of. You just never know. Except, of course, one thing you do know with mum and dad, they always make Christmas really terrific.

If *that* is hope, then the Christian has hope in God. It is a kind of confident expectation. But it is a confidence that never knows for certain how it is going to be answered. It doesn't need to.

This brings me to the next point. Jesus makes some astonishing assertions about prayer. On the other hand, as we saw a little earlier, he assumes certain limitations on it which most of us would unthinkingly ignore. He doesn't pray or counsel us to pray for more than the bare minimum of physical necessities (and even here he reminds us that our heavenly Father knows what we need before we ask him). He doesn't pray that God's judgment should be averted, but only that the edge might be taken off it. And yet on the other hand he says things like, 'If you ask anything in my name, I will do it' (John 14.13). 'All things are possible with God' (Mark 10.27). 'If you have faith no bigger even than a mustard seed, you will say to this mountain, "Move . . .", and it will move; nothing will prove impossible for you' (Matt. 17.20).

The natural man, and the normal Christian, are all too ready to limit their prayers; all too ready to make their own assumptions about what it is and what it is not worth asking; about what God can and what he cannot be reasonably expected to do. But the limits *we* instinctively place on prayer are generally quite

47

different from the ones Jesus places on it, and the possibilities which he sees in it are quite different, and much more far-reaching, than most of us are prepared to credit it with. If we are going to rediscover the meaning of the Christian hope we somehow have to rediscover prayer. At the same time we also have to rediscover the Holy Spirit, and at least there are some signs that the church *is* beginning to rediscover the Holy Spirit. Both of these things, prayer and the Holy Spirit, are concerned with the *possibilities* of the Christian life.

Normally we are all of us too much aware of the *im*possibilities, of the restrictions. William Wordsworth expresses some aspects of this very well. It is something he keeps on coming back to. One way and another he has quite a lot to say about childhood. He doesn't idealize it exactly. But he looks back on it with something like nostalgia. He finds in childhood the origin of poetic vision, of inspiration. But he looks back on it always with a tremendous sense of loss. He looks back on the experiences of childhood and sees in them all, 'fallings from us, vanishings . . .' 'The child is father of the man', true, but the man has lost something that the child took carelessly for granted. 'Whither is fled the visionary gleam? Where are they now, the glory and the dream?'

Wordsworth expresses something that strikes a chord in very many people's hearts. Again, without idealizing childhood; without pretending that their own childhood was deliriously happy; without denying that the child too has griefs and disappointments no less bitter for being seen in more philosophical perspective by the adult, they nevertheless see their adult lives as a continual narrowing of possibilities. Every decision we ever make forecloses certain options for the future. Even the fourteen-year-old choosing his O levels learns that.

All of us, even if we do not take this rather regretful

(or even resentful) view of our life histories, have spent much of our lives coming to terms with ourselves, learning what sort of things it just isn't worth while for *us* to try to do. How many unfortunate experiences did it take to convince you that you are *not* the kind of person who can, let us say, tell funny stories; handle children; organize anything or anybody; keep out of debt? How long did it take you to come to terms with the fact that you would never be popular? That you are not really very good-looking? That as a husband you're a bit of a washout? What we call 'becoming more mature' is to a considerable extent a question of learning to live with our own limitations, of coming to terms with the restrictions placed upon us by our own personalities (like the things I have just mentioned); by things in the past which we had no choice about (like the way we were brought up, for example, and the kind of education we had); and by things that most of us did have some choice about but might find it very hard indeed to alter now (like the career we embarked on, the person we married, the place where we came to live).

Some of us find some of the limitations hard to accept. We have all met the man who really can't tell funny stories, but will insist on trying. We have met the man soured by resentment because he hasn't 'got on' in his job, whose real trouble is that he hasn't come to terms with his own limited abilities. We have met the woman whose marriage was a mistake, but who can't bring herself to admit it, even to herself. We are all familiar with the parents who simply can't be reconciled to the fact that their child is really not specially bright. These are perhaps some of the more striking and obvious instances, but we all do it, over some things. We can't accept the facts about ourselves. We rebel against them, banging our heads against them, making fools of ourselves in the process. We insist on acting as if they weren't there.

And yet, on the other hand, there are many limitations which we are only too ready to accept. There are things we assume we couldn't do, though we've never actually tried. Or we accept *other people's* assumptions about us and respond to *their* ideas about our limitations. All of us constantly allow our future to be thus determined by our expectations, and by other people's expectations for us.

In recent years sociologists and educationists have been making rather a lot of this point. Allocate a child to a certain sort of school, they observe, and you have probably allocated him his station in life. 'What, me! Go to university! You must be joking. People from *our* school don't go to university.' Or put him in a D stream and treat him like a D streamer and the chances are you will get D stream work out of him, whatever his native ability. Your expectations have effectively determined his achievement, because he has allowed your expectations for him to become *his* expectations for himself. When he comes to leave school he will think only in terms of certain sorts of jobs. Others, which may in fact be within his capabilities, will remain beyond his horizon. Many of us thus have our possible careers determined for us by the very streets we were brought up in and the communities from which we emanated. We just accept the pigeon holes into which the educational system and our society thrust us. Home, school, friends and acquaintances, all combine and reinforce each other to confine our image of ourselves, our expectations for ourselves, our assessment of ourselves into certain grooves, and to restrict the possibilities of life.

So then, whereas in some directions we are inclined to rebel against limitations that are all too real, in other directions we are all too ready to come to terms with limitations that either are not, or need not be, there. To get out of this cage which we have built round ourselves, or allowed other people to build round us, isn't an easy thing. Those who do it need a certain heroic quality. My daughter Katherine recently drew my attention to a book which is a first-class commentary on the point I am making. It is by Ivan Southall and is called *Let the Balloon Go*. It is an extraordinarily exciting and sensitive book and I recommend it confidently to any reader between the ages of 9 and 109. It is about a boy who climbs a tree. That's all.

He happens to be a spastic boy. But, as he says himself, inside him there's another, red-blood boy struggling to get out. Well, he gets out. And he climbs a tree. He gets out because he refuses to be told what is possible for him and what isn't.

All of this, of course, is talking about *human* possibilities. Some of our coming to terms, some of our acceptance of our limitations, is necessary and proper. Some of it is mistaken. Some of it is tragic. But accepting the possibilities God sets before us does not involve denying the reality of human incapacities. Faith has nothing to do with pretence. As to the past, faith does not mean pretending that we have no regrets. As to the future, it is not pretending that we have no worries. As to the present, it is not pretending that we have no limitations. If a man is going to avail himself of the possibilities of God he has got to come to terms with human limitations right away. It is a prerequisite of entering into the possibilities of God that we recognize that it is not only in our *in*abilities that we are doomed, but in our abilities too; that not only in the things we can't

51

do, but even in the things we are supremely good at, we fall short of the glory of God; that *at our human best* we fail to fulfil what we might be. Certainly we cannot, just by thinking about it, 'switch over' to success. We can only let our failures be absorbed and transmuted by the success of Christ.

No one denies that it is difficult to open oneself up to what God offers, because in the nature of the case it is a leap into total darkness; because in our human world, bounded by our human horizons, we cannot know what those possibilities are.

Let me again resort to an illustration. It is one which I find peculiarly helpful. Just stop reading. Sit quite still. And try to imagine what it feels like to be an unborn baby.

The psychologists and other wise men of our time tell us that there is really no doubt at all that the unborn baby is conscious. What is he conscious *of*? He is capable, they tell us, of sensation. What sort of sensations does he feel? He is certainly capable of movement, movement which any mother will tell you is a lot less restricted than you might imagine. But it is fairly confined movement all the same.

Try to imagine what he feels. He is warm. But he doesn't know he is warm, because he has never experienced anything else. From the moment he came into existence the temperature around him has never been anything but an unvarying 98.4° F. He is surrounded by the protective cushion of his mother's body — but he has no idea what it is protecting him from. If he *feels* anything it must be simply this constant surrounding pressure and cushioning. He cannot see. He cannot smell. He *can* evidently hear, for he can be shown to respond to sounds, but it is fairly obvious that his hearing must be a somewhat muffled faculty. He has the capacity to feel pain, but it is unlikely that anything has ever hurt him.

So there he is, knowing only the most limited of movements, the most limited of sensations. He has as yet no way of imagining even what it is like to breathe or to eat, to see or to smell, much less to run, to read, to swim, to love, to be afraid.

Supposing you could communicate with this creature and try to explain to him what life was going to be like after he was born, how would you go about it? How *could* you go about it? There is nothing in his world to give him any hint that life can ever be more than he has already experienced, nothing that your explanations could latch on to to convey even the vaguest notion of what he has so far missed. To imagine cold is beyond him. To imagine sight or taste is outside his capabilities. To imagine love or terror without having felt these things would be totally impossible. You might make a start by talking about unrestrained movement. Movement, at least, is something he knows about already. But could you explain 'unrestrained' to him who has never known anything but restraint? Or what about sounds? These at least do come to him from the world beyond. But since he cannot co-ordinate them with anything that he sees or touches, how could he interpret their significance? What could you say to convince him that they even *came* from a world beyond?

If you could talk to him about birth, and persuade him of its inevitability, how could he interpret *that*, except as the end of life as he knew it? You could not make birth sound, to him, like anything except death. Your contention that there was a life beyond it would sound hollow, where it was not unintelligible. He would have no difficulty thinking up a hundred reasons why it could not be so. He might plausibly conclude that this

53

other life was an invention, to help him face less fearfully the unpleasant, inevitable fact of birth, but that in truth, when you're born you're done for.

How wrong can you be? And yet his conclusions, his unwillingness to believe in your descriptions of what was possible for him, of the experience that would be his, some day, is so *reasonable*. It is precisely because they *are* still only possibilities, things he hasn't yet even begun to experience, that he can't be convinced. They are as yet outside his world, or rather, he is outside theirs. — And yet there again, he isn't *really* outside our world, only insulated from it. If he only knew it, the larger world is all around him, there on the other side of a thin wall of flesh, and he only waiting to be born into it.

Everything that has happened to him so far has been a preparation for these very possibilities. The equipment for most of them is already there, waiting to come into action. His eyes are ready to open, though we aren't sure how much he makes at first of the patterns of light and colour that fall on them. They're in full working order, but he'll have to learn to use them. His hearing is there, though again we don't know how discriminating it is when he is first born. His digestive system is there too, and will very shortly after birth begin to make its insistent demands. From the moment of birth he is capable of emotion. He is certainly capable of being frightened. The machinery for other abilities, sitting up, crawling, walking, and eventually doing much more complicated things, will take a little longer to mature, but the basis of it is there. Every muscle he will ever have is already formed. Packed in that dispropor-tionately large head are brain cells which have so far been put to very little use, but which will through the next seventy or eighty years enable him to learn and to accomplish things as yet beyond his comprehension. It is all there, already, and he doesn't know what is in him or conceive what world it is meant to equip him for.

Is it not at least thinkable that the gap between life as we so far know it, and life as it might be, could be as great for us as for that baby? Is it not conceivable that our understanding of what is possible for us might be as limited, and as erroneous, as his?

There is a creature which lives, if I remember rightly, somewhere in south or central America, and which rejoices in the name of the axolotl. It is a kind of tadpole which, if it ever grew up, would be a salamander. But unless some interfering researcher captures it and gives it an injection of thyroid extract the axolotl never does grow up. It lives, grows, even breeds and dies, without maturing, without ever knowing what it might have been. It lives its life in water, whereas if it grew up it could live in air. It's an interesting case of arrested development. The biologists explain that the axolotl evolved that way because immaturity had a survival value. To put it plainly, it's safer for the axolotl to stay a tadpole and to stay in the water. It increases its chances of staying alive by staying immature. I daresay it does. All the same, if *I* were an axolotl I'd want to take the risk. After all, it would be quite an experience.

Or would I? *Do* I?

The anaology, of course, breaks down. The axolotl hasn't really any choice. Nature made him that way and nobody ever told him about hormones. The baby hasn't any choice either. He'll get born. Nature, God willing, will see to that too. But I have a choice. Whether I am born again into the possibilities of God, into the new age; whether I grow up to mature manhood, measured by the full stature of Christ, will depend on my taking certain decisions.

55

I seem to be resorting to analogies a lot. I'm not apologizing; I find them useful. But let me try another one that in some respects is closer to our position. Last holiday I was watching seagulls nesting on a Dorset cliff. They were almost vertical white cliffs, with tiny ledges on which the nests were built, and they fell about three hundred feet into the sea. What does it feel like to be a seagull and to be born in a place like that? Imagine yourself sitting up in your carry cot at a few months old and looking over the edge and seeing nothing but the sea three hundred feet below you. And on the other side of your cot the rock goes straight up to the sky. What do you feel like? The real answer, of course, is that you don't mind a bit. You feel fine. You take it for granted that this is a natural place to live. And so it is.

The young seagull grows and thrives there, on his little ledge, with just about enough room to turn round. That little nest is his world, for the time being, and for the time being every instinct he possesses conspires to keep him in it.

And then he has to leave it. He has to fly. And this is where it must be a very exciting and a very brave thing to be a seagull, because he can't practise.

The seagull can't try out his wings. He can't make short experimental flights. He can't do any preliminary work at nice, safe heights, to get used to the idea. He's there, three hundred feet above the sea, and when he goes, he's got to go.

At some point his bird brain has got to take a real decision. He's got to leave his ledge and go out over the abyss. And until he does it he doesn't know whether he can do it at all. Does the young seagull *really believe* that the air will hold him up? Whether he does or not, at some point he has got to act as if he did. Even if he has no faith he must make the leap of faith, otherwise there is no future for him. But when he does make it, he must know in that very instant that this is where he really belongs, and that all the possibilities are his.

This chapter started off with the New Testament, but it seems to have got a long way from the subject, though I suppose you could say that the bit about the baby has something to do with the new birth.

I don't know, though. It seems to me that what I am trying to say is what the New Testament is saying, too, that the possibilities of God cannot be bounded by our human horizons, that we have too well-defined ideas about what is possible, about what is conceivable and what is not. Without this dimension of openness, of openness to God's possibilities, Christianity is just so many barren ideas in the head, or a collection of so many rather dull observances. And all too often this is exactly what we make of it. Because these possibilities are so difficult to talk about it's hard to convince people that they are there. And because to throw ourselves on the possibilities of God is so *unsafe* a thing to do it is for much of the time more comfortable to ignore them anyway.

Those of us who are in Christ have an enormous responsibility here. You can't blame the outsider for being unaware of the possibilities. But those of us who are inside know that they are real. None of us, except for the saints, really knows very *much* about them, but we've seen enough to convince us that they are there. Yet for most of the time we treat these things like a guilty secret.

I have come back, as one always must in theology, to the difficulty of putting into words what we see and know. And the answer is one that we all recognize — that in the end all the talking is second best. If one man gets assassinated because he's doing what he thinks a

Christian ought to do, then he makes a statement about atonement more powerful than all the sermons that were ever preached on it and all the books of theology that were ever written. If one saint genuinely gives up everything and does the impossible for Christ (and it's going on all the time) he likewise makes a statement about the Holy Spirit and about the possibilities of God.

And if the rest of us, who as yet fall short of either martyrdom or sanctity, want, as it were, to associate ourselves with these statements, we must likewise do it in act, in Christian behaviour and in sacrament (which belong together, I think). We must doubtless go on trying to say what we mean, but it is more important, both for the world and for ouselves, to do what we mean. We must accept what Christ is offering us, which is always more, so much, much more than it looks, and so much, much more than we could imagine.

To take part in a sacrament is to do, to enact, what Christian life is all about. It is to accept, to receive what is offered. To live Christ is not to screw onself up to great heights of moral endeavour and self-sacrifice. It is to accept, to accept what God says is possible for us. This is the achievement, the only achievement for a Christian, to become open to what God offers and what God can do.

4

A Future for the World

Acceptance of the future does not mean accepting any *particular* future as inevitable. If we read the prophets we find that though they have something to say about inevitability they have a lot more to say about *choice*. Man has a choice about his future. It may not always be the kind of choice he would like. It is never a choice without restraints. (It is usually restricted, to start with, by choices he has made in the past.) The future is not something we can mould to our hearts' content, but it is *a future that we can do something about.*

The Christian looks at the past and accepts responsibility for it. He admits that if he had chosen otherwise then things would be different. He looks at the future and he accepts responsibility for that, too. He acknowledges that up to a point it will be what he makes of it. Again, the Old Testament prophet is his guide. The prophet spends his life predicting what is going to happen. But the only reason he bothers to predict the future at all is so that something can be done about it in time. There is thus no question for the Christian of *passive* acceptance of what the future brings. If he has securely grasped his gospel he is never tempted into

59

fatalism, into quietism, into withdrawal from any attempt to influence what comes.

If we turn from the prophets to the New Testament, we find the same attitude, but expressing itself differently. The New Testament is heavy with the sense of destiny. Everything that happens to Jesus, and everything that he does, takes place because 'it was written of him'. It was planned like that. That was how God meant it to be. And yet we are left in no doubt at all that this destiny of Jesus was a destiny which he could have refused at any point. What happened was how it was meant to be, not how it was bound to be. Maybe it's true that God had written the script, but the principal actor wasn't obliged to accept the part. And having accepted it, there was nothing but his own resolution to prevent his walking off the stage. For us, too, there is a future *as it is meant to be*, but it will be up to us whether it ever happens. It will happen only if we grasp the future God offers us as Jesus grasped his, and the only reason there is any hope of our having the courage to do it is that he did it first.

But so far we have talked mostly as if our future were an individual thing, and we all know that this is not entirely so. Many of the choices that determine our future will not be our individual choices at all, but the choice of our government and other people's governments; the choices of civil servants and of business men; the choices of the people at the town hall and of our employers; the choices, in short, of our society, our civilization, our world.

The New Testament has surprisingly little to say about choices of this order, about politics. The reasons are understandable. In the world of the New Testament the important decisions, the ones that affected the future of society, were taken by a relatively small class of rulers and influential people. And the people who wrote the New Testament and those for whom they wrote it didn't belong to this class. If the Old Testament is more politically oriented than the New it is partly because the people who wrote it and at least a few of those to whom it was addressed were genuinely in a position to make political choices. The Old Testament, broadly speaking, is addressed to a nation, which possessed, or lived in hopes of possessing, the power to govern its own affairs. The New Testament is aimed at quite a different kind of community.

We ourselves are nearer the Old Testament situation than the New. We live in what we call democracies, which means that at least in principle we have the power to influence political decisions. We are all involved in politics, if only at the rudimentary level of voting at general elections or arguing about it in pubs. We live in countries where governments cannot totally ignore public opinion. And *we are* public opinion. There is nothing to stop us getting more deeply involved if we really want to. We can join a political party. We can try to get ourselves elected to the local council, or even parliament. If we are prepared to put in the time and the energy, and aren't too much put off by the occasional nastiness of political life, we too can take part in real decision-making.

All this amounts to a substantial difference between our position and that of New Testament men. We have a degree of control over the future of our society which was denied them, and we cannot shirk the responsibility of using it. Some people, somewhere, are deciding the future of our world. Men of God have an obligation to make their voices heard among them. The Old Testament prophets rarely had decision-making power. But they had a voice. They knew it wouldn't always, perhaps wouldn't often, be listened to. But they knew they had no alternative but to speak. We are the prophets in our generation.

When it comes to the practicalities and the details of political life, the man of God has no guarantee of being always right. His main job is to make sure that the politician doesn't lose sight of the ideals, doesn't forget what he's there for. But this doesn't mean that the Christian shouldn't get involved in the practicalities too. If one doesn't *know* about the practicalities, one's ringing call to remember the ideals can often sound unconvincing.

Therefore the Christian must not be a man who plays his football from the terraces; who stands there on Saturday afternoon yelling to the players what they ought to be doing. The Christian must be one who goes on to the field and makes his blunders for himself, or scores his own goals on occasion. I'm not suggesting that *all* Christians ought to rush off and join political parties, but I'm convinced we shouldn't *all* be sitting on the sidelines.

If we have a hope for the future it must *include* a political hope. If you don't like the word 'politics', let me put it another way: if we have a hope for the future it must include some sort of vision of what the world ought to be like and how society ought to be run. But that's politics.

Christians have all too often been repelled by what they see as the nastiness of political life and have been too prone to search for salvation in the cloisters, or among pitch-pine pews on Sunday evenings. If salvation is worth anything, it has to have a political dimension, a secular dimension, a wordly dimension. St Paul, or whoever wrote the epistle to the Colossians, said that 'God was in Christ reconciling the cosmos to himself.'

62

He doesn't say 'reconciling *your soul*', or '*my soul*', but 'reconciling the cosmos'. You can't get a much broader vision than that. There are no half measures about the New Testament's hope for the future. It is a hope for everybody and everything on the earth, and if there are any creatures up there in outer space the hope for the future involves them too. 'Cosmos', the man said, not 'earth'.

One of the merits of the apocalyptists was that they grasped this, the thoroughgoing nature of God's future. They saw God's plan for the future as a cosmic plan. The apocalyptists' fallacy was that they were tempted to write off the present, to devalue the present struggle. They looked at the nastiness of politics and they said, 'God can't do much with this. He must shatter it to bits and start again.' But if we look back into the Bible, behind the apocalyptists, back to the book of Genesis and the story of creation, we find that this is just what God doesn't do. He made a good world, but something went wrong. A whole series of things went wrong. Every time God had a contingency plan somebody went and mucked it up. He planned an idyllic society on South-Sea-island pattern, where man had everything he wanted with only a minimum of work. Man and the serpent between them ruined it. He planned a society based on hard work and a fair division of labour, fair division between men and women, between cattle-keepers and agriculturalists. There was murder. He planned an urban society based on developing technology. Men started building tower blocks and using their technology to challenge his control of the world.

Only once in this story is God tempted to shatter it to bits and start again; and he soon regrets it. What we learn from it is that making the best of things is a divine activity. You and I may be tempted, cynically, to despair of politics, but God hasn't written the politicians off yet. And here we see why. The politicians are men after God's own heart. He's the great pragmatist. He is prepared always to start with things as they are. He himself is the arch-politician, the greatest-ever exponent of the art of the possible. And every time something goes wrong he can be relied on to think of an even better plan — not a better way of reaching the same ideal, but a better ideal.

The Christian must be careful, therefore, that his hope for the future never becomes one that devalues the present. His hope for the city of God must not be one that denies the usefulness of the political struggle in this world. He is not entitled to lose faith in the processes of history or the processes of politics. The ultimate faithlessness is to look at things as they are and to say, 'God can't do anything with this lot'. For it is always with things as they are that God starts, and it may please God, through the nastiness of politics, to save the world he has made. As far as politics is concerned the Christian is a realist. He blinks none of the facts, about human nature, about the corruption consequent on power, about what is achievable, about the limitations of political action. He knows that God was crucified by politicians. Realism, therefore, is commanded. But cynicism and disillusion are forbidden.

What are politicians after all? Only people. People trying to organize each other. People exercising power. And their shortcomings are the common shortcomings of humanity. And if they fail time and time again, it is because humanity fails time and time again. And if they keep coming back for more it is because humanity keeps coming back for more. For the most surprising thing about humanity is its capacity to be surprised by the obvious, by what common experience should have led it to expect. It displays a touching faith that 'things will be better next time', because it never quite gets used to its own weaknesses. The Christian has no illusions about its weaknesses. They are all documented there in the Bible. Yet he has hope above all men; not complacent hope, like the hope that everything will be marvellous when the revolution comes; not cynical hope, like the conviction that the next government at least can't be worse than the one we've got; but a hope that sees that though failures are inevitable, yet after every failure man is summoned to something better. He is not summoned to have just one more try, to employ just one more expedient; to try just one more policy, make one more compromise and hope it works this time. He is summoned instead to aim for something better than he has envisaged before. His very failures become the material of his hopes.

What the Christian has to contribute to political life is vision and compassion, which issue in what looks like a paradoxical combination of passionate involvement and near-infinite detachment. The Christian cannot see or hear of injustice or distress anywhere in the world without his feelings tearing at him to do something about it, *now*. And he believes with all his soul that God feels exactly the same. And yet he also knows that to God, 'sitting on the rim of the universe' as the prophet put it, and watching the generations pass, 'a thousand years are but as yesterday when it is gone, and as a watch in the night'. And the Christian shares some of that detachment.

His expectation for the future, therefore, can never be one which sees the present struggle as an end in itself. He cannot be one of those who are so bound up with the pragmatic realities of the situation that they see no further than this year's balance of payments. But equally he cannot join with those whose eyes are set so firmly on the horizon that they are prepared to trade injustice now for the sake of justice later, and buy their hope of beautiful tomorrows at the cost of other people's misery. The believer has faith to spend his life selflessly to make the world a better place for his children and his children's children for the umpteenth generation. He has faith to accept with equanimity the thought that the world might end tomorrow. For God has given him the task of doing something about his future, and at the same time warned him that the future may at any moment be taken out of his hands. The task does not entitle him to behave as though he were here for ever. The warning is not an invitation to act irresponsibly.

Hope without responsibility has been the prerogative of the millennarians throughout the ages. It is not a truly Christian thing. The Christian hope does not mean leaving it all to God. The Christian's hope does not absolve him from the job of doing something about his future and the future of his world. And doing something about it involves work and it involves suffering. If idealism means always expecting the best, then the Christian is no idealist. If it means not being prepared for how brutal it all is, the Christian is no idealist. But the Christian *is* an idealist if it means never giving up hope, never abandoning faith in the values with which he began. If the Christian is an idealist, he is an idealist in a world where he knows idealists get crucified. Hope is not the same as shallow optimism. It is not the same as romanticizing the future. The Christian dare not romanticize the future, because if he does his job properly it always contains a cross. But the Christian is never disillusioned about the future, because if he does what God wants of him, it always contains a resurrection and a coming of the Holy Spirit. The Christian can never get away from the cross. If he does, he has lost faith. He carries it around with him. And this is only bearable at all because in a sense the dying has already been done for him; the suffering has already been done for him. What he has to do is to *share* in what has already been accomplished.

In politics, more than in any other area of human activity, we live by faith. No man can survive long in the political arena unless he has faith that the sordid realities before him are not the only realities. The Christian engaging in politics begins with no illusions about human institutions or about human nature. And yet he accepts, even asserts, that it is *through* human institutions and human nature that God's will is to be done in the world.

The Christian in politics is no more efficient than the next man; his judgment is no more reliable; he is as prone to miscalculation. What he has to contribute is first of all his integrity. Others, besides Christians, are men of integrity. And for this we should thank God. But a man who has grasped Christian realities *cannot be other* than a man of integrity. He also has to contribute his resolution and commitment. What I mean is this, that the Christian is not the kind who quits easily when the going gets rough. The Christian should also be the man more likely than most to get his priorities right, to remember what he is supposed to be there for. He should be the last to allow the end to justify the means.

But the Christian's attitude to the future should itself give him something that is very valuable in political life. It is a certain quality of imagination, a willingness not to rule out difficult things in advance. If the future is God's future, then we can never come to harm (real harm) by doing what God approves. There may be suffering *now*, but the real interests of the future will be served. The Christian is willing to risk the suffering and the abuse, now, for the sake of what is to come. He is willing to face the wilderness, and to lead others through the wilderness, for the sake of the promised land.

Whenever one raises the question of Christian involvement in politics, someone is sure to observe that Christians in politics don't always take the same side. The implication is always that this is a difficulty, an embarassment. If Christians really had any political answers, wouldn't they agree about what they are?

There is really no reason why they should. One doesn't expect all Christians to like the same books, or enjoy the same entertainers. In matters of taste faith does not make very much difference. Neither does it make much difference in matters of practical judgment. Two Christian gardeners would not necessarily agree about the best time to prune roses. Why should two Christians necessarily agree as to whether it is a good idea to nationalize the banks? All Christians would agree that what we want is a just society, but there is not only *one* possible just society. Some Christians are convinced that a socialist society would be more likely to be just than a conservative one. Others foresee that a socialist society would be likely to be *less* just, at least in the ways that they care about most. What divides these two sets of Christians is a purely technical political judgment about the best way of getting a just society.

I doubt whether any Christian feels that our society at the moment works entirely satisfactorily. We would all like to see improvements. Most Christians, I imagine, take the view that by working away at the system we could make such improvements. It would doubtless never become perfect, but we could approximate more

68

nearly than we do now to the just society which we all hope for. Not only conservative Christians but the majority of socialist ones share this standpoint. Socialist and conservative disagree about the extent of the necessary changes, and such disagreements are serious enough, but they mostly agree that what is needed is some *reform* of our existing structure, not its replacement with something different.

Now it is quite possible to take a different view. There are those who argue, more radically, that our existing structures *never can* produce the just society, and that to play about trying to reform them is a waste of time. The capitalist system, they say, is *inherently* unjust, because it is ultimately founded on exploitation, albeit sometimes paternalistic exploitation. To aim at justice by reforming the existing order is therefore to attempt the impossible, or the self-contradictory, because a prerequisite for achieving justice is the destruction of the existing order.

Such a view as I have here set out is manifestly uncongenial, at the present time, to the majority of Englishmen, whether Christian or not. I set it out simply to show that it is not *less Christian than* the alternatives. It differs in purely technical respects. Whether the capitalist system is inherently incapable of producing justice is not a moral question, or a religious question; it is a matter of technical political judgment.

Christianity does not prescribe particular political solutions. Christians may be found at virtually any point on the poltical spectrum. This only becomes harmful or dangerous when a Christian gets his political and religious judgment confused, or becomes so blinkered politically that he cannot see how another Christian can take any other political standpoint than his own. This happens very easily, of course. I know a number of

Christian socialists who admit that they cannot really see how a Christian can be other than a socialist. I know some Christian conservatives who just cannot conceive how anyone who calls himself a Christian can do anything so dangerous and disruptive as to advocate the otherthrow of the social order.

The identification of Christianity with our own chosen political ideals is even easier in the case of ideals which most of us happen to share. All of us in the West believe in democracy. Anyone who doesn't is usually well advized to keep quiet about it. As a consequence there is a very general assumption that democracy is the most Christian form of social order, and that any threat to democracy is a threat to Christianity. Now this is nonsense, as even the briefest look at history will show. If there is any natural affinity between Christianity and democracy, it took the church an astonishingly long time to discover it. Until relatively recent times most men regarded democracy itself as a threat to Christianity. A president of the Methodist church (admittedly it is a generation or two ago) once went on record as saying that 'Methodism is as much opposed to democracy as to sin.'

I am not here advocating a return to totalitarianism. I hope I am as good a democrat as the next man. I think that with all its drawbacks (which are real) the virtues of democracy far outweigh those of any realistic alternative. But I use this illustration in order to convince any who remain doubtful that there really is no necessary tie-up between Christianity and any political system whatever. There are doubtless some forms of political order which are inherently so unjust that no Christian could willingly support them; but if we exclude these we are still left with a great many possibilities.

There *are* political ideals about which Christians must

agree, but they are concerned not with particular forms of social order but with ways in which the social order works. The Bible has nothing to say about democracy. It tends to take for granted whatever forms of social order were current at the time of writing. It has a great deal to say about justice. Whatever the form of social order, the will of God is that it should work justly.

Now there is nothing specifically Christian or biblical about the ideal of justice. For this we may be thankful. Most other men share our reverence for it, at least in theory. What should distinguish the Christian is the depth of his devotion and the extent of his commitment to the common ideal.

One question which did not apparently occur to the Christians of early times is whether there can ever be a Christian duty actually to defy the ruling power. Most Christians of later times, with their devotion to the *status quo*, would have reacted with horror and outrage even to the suggestion that there might be such a duty. But for our own age the question is an inescapable one. If a law is unjust, and cannot be changed by lawful means, is there a Christian obligation to disobey the law? If a government is unjust, is there a Christian duty to work for the overthrow of the government? If a state is unjust, with an unjust constitution, should a Christian oppose it even with violence, if that proves the only way to oppose it effectively?

If as Christians we are seriously concerned with the future of our world we cannot simply ignore such questions as these. They may not be our questions, but they will be relentlessly asked for us by others. The will of God for his world is order. The will of God for his people is justice. But what if we cannot get justice without making disorder?

I do not know the answers to these questions. I know

what I should *like* to answer. I should like to answer that violence is a human short-cut that never really arrives at the destination to which it is meant to lead; that those who take the gun perish by the gun; that in the long run the only true way is to suffer violence, not to do it. But I am not entitled to give this answer, because it is not my problem. I am not entitled to sacrifice other men's claims for justice on the altar of my non-violent ideals. I have no right to demand suffering from other men. Only those who suffer have the right to espouse non-violent solutions.

The Christian's role in working out the future of the world is to be relentless in his pursuit of justice for other men. In an earlier chapter I said that our perspective on the future was moulded by the fact that we no longer had to worry about where the next meal was coming from, or about the possibility of going to the workhouse. This is true, but in any consideration of the future of the *world* we have to take account of the very large numbers of people who still do; of the vast numbers for whom there isn't even the workhouse to fall back on. For ourselves a poor harvest means a few price rises in the shops. We need to consider those for whom a poor harvest is a first-order disaster, and three poor harvests in a row mean probable death. The future for the world involves the future of our own poor, whose problems we tend to ignore precisely because they aren't typical any more, and because too many of us take glibly for granted that everyone these days has two cars and a colour telly. There are not inconsiderable numbers in our own cities who worry about the possibility of finding themselves with nowhere to live. If we are to speak about the future without hypocrisy, what we say must include their future, too.

When one talks about the Christian's attitude to the

future, it is so easy to concentrate on his attitude to his own individual future. And then one talks about 'be not anxious' and 'take no thought for the morrow', and makes the Christian sound like a very unworldly person who takes what comes and isn't bothered; who trusts God and then relaxes. And all this is true, but only up to a point. It is true that when one genuinely trusts God one faces the future with an enormous sense of freedom. But it is not the freedom of the man who has contracted out of the struggle. It is not really freedom to relax; not an unworldly freedom. The Christian is not free of responsibility, he is free *for* responsibility. He is free of fear, but not of concern. And all this becomes clear immediately one stops talking about the Christian's own future and asks, 'But what about the future of the world?'

Somewhere near the beginning of this chapter I said that the New Testament's perspective on the future of the world was bound to be somewhat different from our own, because the New Testament writers wrote as men who had no serious opportunity to take political decisions or even influence them. There is another respect in which we differ from them materially. In our days the capacity of mankind to manipulate its environment has increased to a degree that they would have found unimaginable. The future of the world is to a large extent at the mercy of our own technology. This is another reason why our attitude to the future cannot be precisely the same as that of the men of the New Testament. We have a *kind* of control over the future of our world which people in their days did not even dream of, and we cannot contract out of the responsibility for exercizing it.

This raises vast questions which cannot be pursued now, but one point must be made which concerns the

Christian contribution to the discussion of our technological future. It may be briefly put as follows: technology does not, in the last resort, determine the values of society, but is determined, or at least controlled *by* them. Let me explain what I mean by this.

On all hands, but especially in the press, one comes across discussions of our technological future, much of it concerned with the wisdom of promoting this or that project. Should we go on building Concorde? Do we need a third airport? Can we do without urban motorways? And over and over again in such discussions one finds at least some of the protagonists making the assumption that technology has not only a momentum of its own but a sort of inner logic of its own which makes its progress irresistible. If passenger aircraft to travel at Mach 3 *can* be built, then of course they *must* be built. This is 'the logic of aircraft development'. Someone argues that the 70 mph speed limit 'has regrettably distorted motor car design', i.e. (in your language and mine) has discouraged motor car designers from their natural tendency to design ever faster and faster cars. The implication is that such 'distortion' is somehow unnatural and ought not to be allowed. With regard to the motorways we are told that 'the motor car is here to stay', that 'car ownership is bound to become even more widespread'. To resist the driving of motorways through city centres and beauty spots alike is therefore to 'stand in the way of progress'.

Now all this is rubbish. There is no such thing as a 'natural' development of technology. Technology develops in the directions in which human beings *choose* to develop it. There is no law of nature which says that once we have produced an atom bomb we are obliged to go on to develop a hydrogen bomb, and that when we

74

can make a one hundred megaton bomb we cannot stop until we have produced a one thousand megaton bomb. Human communities are quite capable of deciding, and some of them have decided, that though they have the capacity to do so they do not wish to produce nuclear weaponry at all. There is nothing to prevent us putting a stop to particular lines of technological development, and of course we are doing it all the time. We cannot develop everything, even if we wanted to, we haven't the money or resources, so we must all the time be choosing which lines to pursue and which not to pursue.

There is no denying that certain technological developments acquire an impetus of their own. The motor car is the ounstanding example. But to talk as if we are at the mercy of our own technology is ridiculous.

The same idea crops up in another context. On more than one occasion in recent months I have read serious scientific discussions about the possibility of life on other planets or stars elsewhere in the universe. And I have come across a curious argument which some quite sensible scientists apparently find convincing. They calculate the number of heavenly bodies they think are out there, the number on which the conditions necessary for life are, statistically speaking, likely to occur, and the statistical chances of life actually having originated on them. They arrive at a figure which suggests that there are likely to be a number of places, a quite considerable number, where life exists in the universe. Then comes the interesting stage in the argument. Some of these heavenly bodies are likely to have produced conditions suitable for life-formation earlier than our earth did. Life has existed on them for longer than it has here. Allowing x years for the evolution of higher life-forms, y years for the more primitive stages of social and intellectual development, and z years for the development of an advanced technology which would include space travel and communications, we can arrive at a figure indicating the number of civilizations in outer space who are capable of getting in touch with us or whom it is worth our while trying to get in touch with.

Now this argument rests on a number of fascinating assumptions on which I should love to comment, but I restrain myself and confine my attention to the matter in hand. The one assumption that is relevant to our argument is that one can, even approximately, allow y years for the earlier stages of social and intellectual development and postulate that any self-respecting higher life-form would have got round to space travel and other kinds of advanced technology after z years more. The assumption is that such developments are somehow inevitable; that any humanoid or higher life-form is bound to be interested in the same things as we are; that his curiosity is bound to propel him in the same directions; that he is bound to devote himself to the same aims as we have chosen for ourselves.

It is frightening that a scientist should know so little of human history that he can be taken in by an argument of this sort. Human beings have got to where they are because they have made certain choices, accepted certain values. The real determining factor in human progress has never been what was technologically possible, but what we chose to do with the technology at our disposal.

Look, for example, at the Middle Ages. Mediaeval man was no moron. He had as much intelligence as you and I have. He had a technology, a mastery of certain arts and crafts which still must command respect. He couldn't do all the things we can do. But come to that, we can't do all the things he could. But he did not devote his technological expertise, such as it was, to travelling at high speeds, or even to maximizing his agricultural output. He devoted a good deal of it to the building of beautiful cathedrals for the worship of Almighty God.

Now I am not at this point suggesting that he was right and that we are wrong. I merely point out that the real, the vital difference between mediaeval man and ourselves is not the difference between his command of technology and ours. It is the difference between the ends which we have chosen that our respective technologies should serve. We do not find ourselves travelling through the skies at five hundred miles an hour because we happen to have stumbled on the way to do it. We decided that it would be a good idea to travel through the skies at five hundred miles an hour and have accordingly spent a great deal of time and vast amounts of money developing the technology to do it. The men of the Middle Ages developed instead the arts and crafts appropriate to the building of cathedrals because they thought that the worship of Almighty God was the thing most worth spending their time on.

The kind of assumption which I have been examining, that the development of technology is inevitable, is highly dangerous because it fosters the belief that in certain areas we can do nothing, or very little, to alter things, that we have no choice about our future. In this situation the Christian is needed as a prophet. He is not the only prophet, for many others are joining him. He must assert that the future of the world will be to a large extent what the citizens of the world make it. We are not the slaves of our technology. We can choose. We can choose, if we wish, to make our technology serve quite different ends from those it is now mostly serving, and Christians would probably not disagree very much as to what most of those new ends ought to be.

5

A Future for the Church

Any Christian who isn't sickened by the church hasn't yet discovered what the gospel is about. Anyone who has is bound to be disgusted by all sorts of features of church life; with the triviality of so much of it; with the way the people running the show manage to forget for so much of the time what they are supposed to be running it *for*; with the way the church is preoccupied with *itself*. In this last respect the flourishing and the declining churches are exactly alike. Each is busy contemplating its own navel, the one in self-congratulation, the other in self-pity. Nobody who knows the church from inside needs to wonder why so few people nowadays attend it. The wonder is that anybody bothers to go at all.

I could go on like this for pages, and all of it would be true. I won't. The reader is invited to add his own expansion. I've no doubt you all can.

Has the church a future? Whether it has or it hasn't, few of us can have any doubts as to whether it deserves one.

But let us not be too contemptuous — for two reasons. First, if I criticize the church I have to end up

78

by admitting: 'Yes, of course it's all true. The church is rotten. And you're part of it. And it's as much your responsibility as anybody else's. If you can see so much that's wrong, get in there and do something about it. And if you're not prepared to, then stop pretending that you care so much about it.'

Second, we can all see how any institution, founded for whatever purpose, can get preoccupied with the simple business of self-perpetuation, the mechanics of keeping itself going. That's the danger. But we can't avoid it by doing away with the institution. As long as there are any believers left they will be a community, i.e. a church. Some *sort* of institution is therefore inevitable. So although we may criticize the church, we are stuck with it in some form or other as long as we are stuck with the gospel. Gospel means people. Faith means community. And people is church; community is church, whatever shape you give it. And as long as you have people, and community, the chores have got to be done.

Look at the family. We'd all like a beautiful, harmonious family life, with beautiful family relationships. But while we're busy building the beautiful life and enjoying the beautiful relationships somebody has to make the dinner and somebody has to do the washing up. And if we can't agree about who or how, then what price the beautiful relationships?

Nobody doubts that these things have got to be done. It's just a matter of not getting them out of proportion. We don't want the family to turn into an organization devoted to the sole end of making dinners and washing up afterwards — though there are housewives, here and there, who in their bitter moments feel that their family has become exactly that.

Similarly with the church: we mustn't become an

organization whose sole task is to keep itself going, but all the same, while the church is doing the really important things, like worshipping God, celebrating the sacraments, preaching the gospel, serving the community, somebody does have to clean the windows and somebody does have to audit the accounts, and the church gives God no glory by neglecting either of these jobs.

But there is more to be said. Go back for a moment to the family. It is not a matter of doing the washing up and making the dinner *in addition to* sustaining the beautiful relationships. The relationships *express themselves in* the way we organize and share out the chores. As all mankind has known since it came down out of the trees, if a family, or any other community, wants to express, preserve or foster a relationship, the most potent way to do it is to make dinner, i.e. to eat a meal together. Getting the dinner made is not therefore an irritating extra, additional to family life. It *is* family life.

Likewise in the church, polishing the floors and getting ready for the bazaar are not irritating extras either. They may be irritating to those who would rather be doing something else, but they are part of the discipline of the spiritual life, as long as they are seen in proper perspective.

Mrs Jones once said, 'I've polished all the church brass, and I've knitted two dozen little woolly dogs for the bazaar, so I think *I've* earned my place in the kingdom of God.' Well, we could all tell Mrs Jones what's wrong with *her* perspective, but in condemning her remember two things: some of us look forward to the revolution, when the present form of the church will be swept away and there will arise a brave, new church, having neither brass nor bazaars. But until that time comes, the brass needs to be polished and the bazaars (I

80

regret this as much as you do) need to be organized. That's one thing. The other is much more important. The church, whether in its brave new form or its unbrave, old form has got a lot of people around whose only discernible talent is for polishing brass and making little woolly dogs. Somehow it has not only to make room for them but to make them feel useful and wanted. To be quite frank, Mrs Jones gets me down rather. We rarely see eye to eye about anything. But if the brave new church has no place for Mrs Jones, and can't use what she has to offer, then I shall regretfully conclude that in some ways the brave new church is worse than the one we have now, and moreover, that the ways in which it is worse are some of the ways that matter most.

We can all construct high-flown theologies that help the Christian trade unionist to relate his faith to his working life, or that tell the Christian industrialist how to employ his money and his power. We might even have a stab at working out a theology that helps car-owning, property-owning suburban man get his values and priorities sorted out; or helps captive suburban woman to stop getting depressed — though that's more difficult. But there would still be a good many people whom these excellent theologies would leave untouched.

If I made a list of all the people connected with my church — if I took a census, say, of everyone who set foot on the premises between midnight Sunday and midnight Sunday next — for a start, most of them would be children, and an awful lot of the adults would be Mrs Jones. So if we want to construct a theology that helps the people we actually *touch* (St Paul did this, you remember, and it turned out to be a theology peculiarly helpful to slaves), then we have to think of one that is

81

useful to Jane, who is in class 3G at the local primary school and comes to Brownies and Sunday School, and which makes sense to Roger, who is in the lower sixth and is second reserve striker for the school football team, and *very* occasionally comes to youth fellowship. A theology that is worth anything can't afford to leave them out, *and*, somehow or other, somewhere or other, it has also got to fit in these woolly dogs of Mrs Jones's.

It's tempting to ignore them, and most of the books on theology do ignore them. But not the Bible. Look up Acts 9.36f. I always used to think of this as one of the sillier stories of the New Testament, but now I think I see what it is really about. All right; they aren't little woolly dogs, they're little woolly jackets. But the premier apostle, the Rock on which the church was built, was expected to be interested in them. And he was. Perhaps it *is* just a story. Perhaps it never happened. I wouldn't know; but I don't think it matters very much whether it did or it didn't. It's certainly very difficult to believe. The value of the story in Acts 9 about the resurrection of Mrs Jones doesn't depend on whether it happened or not. The story is an assertion of the value of Mrs Jones to the church.

It is very easy to look round at the church and to feel disillusioned. There is plenty that is wrong. It is tempting to conclude that nothing can be done with the church, or for it; that in order to do anything useful we must shatter it to bits and then remould it nearer to the heart's desire. Why don't we start off again from first principles and make a *new* church, or a para-church, or a non-church, or something equally exciting? But while the theological death-or-glory boys are out constructing their para-churches or their non-churches there are those who feel stuck with the one they've got; who cannot see past the people who are there in front of them now, like

82

sheep without a shepherd. And is this a less Christ-like thing? (Mark 6.30-34).

I have a great respect for the theological radicals. I have sympathy for the man who turns his back on the church in disgust and disillusion. I admire the one who goes out on a shoestring of faith into the godless world, accepting the fact that his own brethren call him a betrayer. I respect the man who says in the name of God that God is dead, and that in this world he must be an atheist. But more than all these I respect the man who takes his disillusion in both hands and offers it to God, and goes on doing 'the work that lies under his nose, with the tools that lie under his hand'.

If we are thinking of the future of the church, or wondering whether there *is* a future for the church, the last thing any of us ought to be is complacent. We need a revolution all right. If there is any hope for the church it will appear only when the Holy Spirit has given us all such a shaking that we don't know whether we're inside out or right way up.

And yet — this hope for the future must not be one that devalues what we are doing now, or that writes off as irrelevant the devotion that is now being displayed. Any hope for the future of the church has to start with the people who are now in it; it has to meet their needs and make use of their devotion. Some of our radicals, when they talk about the future of the church, remind me too much of the Irishman who, if he was going to Ballymeena, 'wouldn't start from here'. But we have no alternative but to start from here. And it doesn't seem to be God's habit to start anywhere else. Whether he is dealing with his world or his church, it is with the things as they are that he begins. *He* has hope for his church, and he is inviting us to share it.

But if we are to share his hope, we must be prepared

for *any* eventuality, for God himself is the greatest radical of all. We must be prepared for the possibility of a revolution so comprehensive that it will look like total destruction, for a rebirth that will look frighteningly like death. We must be prepared to question *everything*, for only so can God show us what is essential. We must be prepared for testing, like Abraham, whose hope in God was so secure that he could contemplate the sacrifice of the only thing he understood as hope. You can't be much more radical than that. They say that Abraham is the great example of faith. I sometimes wonder. It says that 'he went out, not knowing . . .' I sometimes fancy that he had left faith far behind; that he was away out on the edge of things, where only a sliver of hope sustains. When we can join him out there on the edge, in hope sacrificing hope — only then may we see light, and be satisfied.

Some people these days see great possibilities for the church in the charismatic movement. They could be right, I suppose; we must rule nothing out. I'm no expert on the charismatic movement. My experience of these people has been very limited. The ones I have encountered impress me with nothing so much as with their narrowness. They seem to have no doctrine of the Holy Spirit. Or if they do, they seem to conceive of his acting only in certain ways, in certain grooves. The only thing we know for certain about the Holy Spirit is that he will surprise us. What he does is always a new thing. He can work, and I'm sure is working, through secular men in the secular world. He can even work through the institutional church, through old, fossilized bodies like the C of E and inefficient bureaucratic machines like Methodism. Perhaps the charismatics are at least part of the shake-up, alarm clocks to wake us up to the fact that the Holy Spirit is not yet dead. All the same, he is more alive than the charismatics themselves imagine. Before the new hope dawns we shall be driven to questionings that will make the radicals of the sixties look like fuddy-duddy conservatives, and we shall be possessed by the spirit in such measure that the charismatics of the seventies will look like men at a funeral tea. But it is unlikely that the church will repeat the triumphs of the past. We should look for no great revivals like the ones of last century, or the ones we saw earlier under Wesley and Whitfield. We shall do greater things than these.

People inside the church at the moment are much prone to depression. Nothing seems to work. We have tried all the old expedients, the things that worked last time, and they have failed us. Of course they have. We are like a dog who has learnt a series of tricks and is disillusioned now that they are no longer rewarded with biscuits.

The things that worked last time were God's gifts to the church for their day and their hour. We must open ourselves to the gifts he is giving, or offering us, now. It is not a matter of giving it just one more try, or attempting to think up yet another gimmick for attracting more people in to fill the pews. We must get back to the beginning and ask very, very basic questions, about what the gospel is really about, and about what matters most. We must be prepared to reconsider everything, to question everything, to scrap anything, however dear to us, if it is not one of the essentials. This is not a plea for revolution for revolution's sake; not a suggestion that we throw things out for the sake of throwing out. It is a plea that we should be prepared to look at everything again. For one of the greatest gifts of the spirit is an open mind. He is the enemy of all dogmatism, all narrowness, all rules and all tradition. He is the flood, the torrent. The church is like a child playing on the beach, throwing up his little ramparts, preparing his little channels to lead the sea, as he fancies, here or there. And then the tide comes in.

And when our tide comes in, and the overflowing flood passes through, our little edifices will not stand, and our little channels, dug whether by catholic or charismatic, will not contain him or his grace. We should not be busying ourselves, as most of us are, devising ways to build a better sandcastle. We should be learning to swim. So that when the tide sweeps through we are not among those who can only see his work as destruction, but are borne up by that flood.

The church, then, must live in hope, and she *can* hope, but it is hope that is the very antithesis of shallow optimism. It is the hope of rebirth, and there's nothing very comfortable about being born. So please don't imagine that I am saying, 'Cheer up! There's life in the old church yet.' Or, 'God will see us through if we only sit tight.' That's not the message. The message is: the opportunity is there, the pearl of great price is before us, if we're prepared to throw away everything in order to get it. The church can be raised to life; if it is prepared to die. This is the message, that things will get worse for the church, and when they get worse, rejoice, because you know that your deliverance is at hand.

6

The Usefulness and the Limitations of Eschatological Language

I hope I have said enough to show that a great deal of what the Bible has to say about the future is not said in eschatological language. Its doctrine of the last things is not by any means the whole of its doctrine of the future. If we want to understand the biblical writers' attitude to the future we must not ignore what they have to say about the last things. But equally, if we wish to understand and appreciate properly their teaching about the last things, we must see it as part of the whole complex of their attitude to the future. To put the matter more simply: the New Testament writers, at least, look at the future, and invite us to do so too, in the light of the possibility that the world might end tomorrow. But they do not allow their view of the future to be totally dominated by that possibility. If anyone were to talk about the future solely in eschatological terms, therefore, as if the possibility of the world's end were the most important single fact to be considered, they would not be presenting a biblical or a Christian view of the future. But equally, if we ignore this possibility altogether, and forget about eschatology entirely, the chances are that we are missing out something important and presenting not a biblical or truly Christian view of the future at all, but a distortion or misrepresentation of it.

Although, therefore, this chapter will be mainly about eschatological language; and although I shall be insisting that such language is still valuable, and trying to draw out those aspects of Christian truth which can be more readily expressed in such language than in any other; I do not mean to imply that eschatological language has no limitations. There are some things which need to be said and which cannot be said in this form. And there are ways of pressing eschatological language to a logical conclusion to which the New Testament authors never meant it to be pressed.

The New Testament church took very seriously the possibility that the world might end at any time. There were certain important ways in which the Christians of that time allowed their behaviour and their attitudes to be influenced by that possibility. But there were other ways in which it might logically have been expected to influence their behaviour but in which they did not allow it to do so.

At first, shortly after the resurrection of Jesus, his followers in Jerusalem were so confident of his early return in glory that they began to live on their capital. This is what lies behind the descriptions of early church life in Acts 4.32-5.11. Natural as this was at the time the church at large seems quickly to have decided that it was an error. It was not the end of the error, even so. The references to idlers and idleness in the Thessalonian correspondence seem to imply that some members of that church had given up their jobs in expectation of the imminent end. The apostle feels moved to lay down the firm, almost brutal-sounding rule, 'If anyone will not work, let him not eat' (II Thess. 3.10).

Here we see the church at work defining what eschatology does not mean. The world may come to an end at any time. Furthermore, it may be added, Jesus said, 'Take no thought for the morrow . . .' Nevertheless, 'If anyone will not work, let him not eat.' Is the apostle suggesting that the expectation is wrong, or contradicting the advice of our Lord? He is doing neither. He is insisting that neither the one nor the other must be understood as an invitation to irresponsibility. There are some conclusions which may look tempting, but which may not legitimately be drawn either from our trust in God or from our expectation of the possible end.

Although the church did not abandon its eschatological hope, therefore, it refused to allow this hope totally to dominate its attitude to the future. Eschatological language could not say everything about the future which it wished to say.

Part of the reason for inserting the two previous chapters on the future of the world and the future of the church was to illustrate this very point. In discussing such matters the Christian is obliged to use some very non-eschatological language. He must not speak of the future of the world or of the church as if the continuance of either were guaranteed, but he must certainly reckon with the strong possibility of their continuing for the time being.

Having warned ourselves thus briefly of the limitations of eschatological ways of talking about the future, let us now look at their positive value.

First, eschatology is a necessary challenge to our complacency. We in the affluent West are a whole generation, a whole civilization, of rich fools taking our ease while our barns are pulled down and the sites redeveloped. More than anything we need the reminder that this very night our souls may be required of us. And we need the reminder because it is literally true, the world *could* end, and certainly our civilization could end, at any time, and for a variety of foreseeable reasons. For some years we have possessed nuclear bombs powerful enough to do the job unaided. But nuclear war apart, we are now aware that the whole environment is a fairly delicately balanced system. The balance in particular places is always tipping this way and that. A small reduction in average rainfall for a few years in North Africa and hundreds of square miles that once supported life become a desert. Men build a dam, the water table rises, and entire populations of plants and animals are wiped out, to be replaced by others. The earth as a whole, the environment of us all, plants, animals and men, may be equally vulnerable to modest-looking changes. A slight rise in the carbon-dioxide level of the atmosphere (well within the capacity of our power stations to produce) or a reduction in the concentration of ozone in the upper air (which our high-flying supersonic jets might possibly be capable of accomplishing) and the climate of the earth might warm up by a fraction, or cool down. Would it matter? We can't be absolutely sure, but it is *possible* that such innocent looking changes could trigger off another ice age, or conversely start a contraction of the polar ice caps that would raise the level of the oceans and flood the major cities of half the world. We don't know for certain just how delicately balanced we are on the knife edge. We do know that the scale of human activities on the earth is now such that we could, without realizing it, in a multitude of possible ways precipitate our own doom.

So much for the possibilities of destruction inherent in our technology. What of the possibilities for destruction inherent in our poltiical and economic organization? We in the West have grown fat by exploiting the impoverished rest of the world. It is beginning to dawn on the impoverished rest what has been going on, and what is still going on. How long until the wretched of the earth arise, realizing that they have nothing to lose but their chains? If they do, it will not be the end of the world in the sense in which a nuclear war would be the end (for the poor themselves, it would be the beginning), but it would be the end of *our* world, the comfortable world that we have built around ourselves, the false world of the rich, complacent few among the multitudes of poor.

One does not need to be a Christian in order to be aware of these possibilities; they are being pointed out to us all the time in the press and on television and elsewhere. But the Christian has a part to play in forcing his fellow men to face up to them, for he preaches a gospel which has always beeen the enemy of human complacency, and which has always stressed that one of the facts men have to take account of in their contemplation of the future is the insecurity of life in this world.

If a growing understanding of our environment has revealed how precariously balanced are the conditions for human life (and indeed any sort of life) on this planet, our growing understanding of human biology, medicine and such like subjects has revealed how delicately poised is the life of the individual organism. The human body is an incredibly complicated but for the most part self-regulating mechanism. The more we learn about its complications the more impressive its capacity for self-regulation becomes, and the more remarkable it appears that for so much of the time the mind-boggling delicacy of its balance is maintained. We all know from experience what unpleasant effects, and what ultimately dangerous effects, can be produced by relatively small increases in our internal body temperatures. From 98.4°F a rise to a mere 100°F is disturbing. A rise to 104°F is alarming. Our health, and in the last resort our life, is dependent on the presence in our diets of nearly undetectably minute traces of elements or queer chemicals that most of us have never heard of. An unbelievably slight alteration in the concentration of the various hormones in our body fluids and our behaviour could become bizarre, or our growth monstrously distorted. That so many living creatures remain healthy and sane is a continuing miracle.

When we consider the further complications of genetics, of the machinery by which the organism produces another organism more or less like itself, our wonder is bound to increase. The odd knot in a chromosome here or there, or a bit of damage to even a few molecules of nucleic acid in the cells from which we grew, and we wouldn't be here at all. The really remarkable thing is not that we survive, but that nature gets it right often enough and for long enough to ensure that so many of us even manage to be born.

One of the results of our increasing knowledge, therefore, is to increase our appreciation of the insecurity of life, both at a global and at an individual level. As a race, and as individuals, we are living permanently on the edge of extinction, at the mercy of forces, vast forces beyond our control and minute forces beyond our comprehension. The language of eschatology, therefore, is in the first place the language of literal truth. Any realistic appraisal of our future must reckon immediately with the fact that our future is not assured. I do not know whether I shall be here tomorrow. I do not know whether the world will be here tomorrow. If I am to act responsibly I must reckon with the strong possibility that both I and it will still be in existence, but if I am tempted to plan for the future on the complacent assumption that I or other human beings have got the future entirely under control, the Bible has a warning for me: 'Fool! this very night . . .'

If we talk about eschatology in this sort of way, if we insist that the world *could* end at any time, that we as individuals *might* not be here tomorrow, we are talking conditionally. We are saying the sort of things about the future that the prophets said. We are much closer to the prophets than to the apocalyptists. The apocalyptists gave the impression that the world was going to end, come what may, because that is the way God had planned it. The prophets were more inclined to say that the world might end, or the world as they knew it might end, *if* men continued to behave as they were. And this was not so much because God planned that it should happen but because he would allow it to happen, because it is one of his rules than humanity must live with the consequences of its own actions.

The apocalyptists' message might be summed up as 'Prepare to meet your doom.' The prophets' was, 'Prepare to meet your doom, unless . . .' If we are to stand within the main stream of biblical thinking we must make room for that 'unless . . .'

If we use eschatology in the way in which I have been suggesting, we are also fairly close to the main stream of biblical thinking in another respect. A nuclear war, we might say, would be the end of the world. It would not necessarily mean the total end of the planet, however, or of human life upon it. What survived of human society would most likely be an almost unrecognizable fragment of what exists now, but something might survive. We do not really compromise the seriousness of our threat of an end by admitting such a possibility. Similarly, an environmental disaster might not totally wipe out all human life. The other possible 'eschatological' event which we envisaged, the overthrow of Western civilization, certainly would not do so. If we are put to it, therefore, we have to admit that our 'eschatology' does not necessarily imply the absolute and total termination of the world and what is in it. Most of the Bible uses its 'eschatology' in the same way. If it speaks of an 'end', it does not necessarily mean that there will be more human history, that creation will be undone. It may occasionally mean that, but generally the 'end' is no more than the end of a chapter. Even at that, it is usually a pretty decisive end. It necessitates a very fresh start, but it does not assert that a fresh start is inconceivable. A realistic eschatology must be realistic in this sense too. If we describe a nuclear war as 'the end of the world', 'the end of civilization' or 'the end of life as we know it', few will quibble about our choice of words. But we must not deny the possibility that even beyond *that* event there might eventually be hope.

If, then, we speak eschatologically about the future we are speaking no more than sober realism, but eschatological language has a wider function than this. It can afford us ways of expressing certain attitudes to, and convictions about, both the future and the present, attitudes and convictions which can be expressed more readily and forcefully in eschatological language than in any other terms. I shall devote the rest of this chapter to exploring what these things are that can be better said in eschatological language than in any other.

1. To speak eschatologically is a way of indicating the things to which one attaches supreme importance; or rather, a way of conveying what supreme importance one attaches to the things indicated. Supposing someone

94

tempts me to commit an act of serious dishonesty. How do I reply? I might say that I was afraid of being caught. I might protest that my reputation would suffer, or my public image be tarnished. I might plead the constraints of my own conscience, and say that my *self*-esteem, my self-respect would be damaged, and that remorse would keep me awake at nights. I might conceivably fall back on the moral law, and simply quote the ten commandments at my tempter. Or I might say to myself (it would sound pretentious if I said it to anyone else), 'If I do this, how shall I stand before God?'

Now that last argument is an eschatological one, and it says something which none of the others say. It says that how I act in this situation before me is more than just a matter of worldy consequences; more than the sanctions of my own conscience; more than a question of moral principle. Or perhaps it is saying that this *is* a question of moral principle and is trying to indicate of what overwhelming importance I consider moral principles to be. It is saying that the moral principle here is not just a matter of conscience; it is not even just a matter of life and death. It is a matter of eternal significance. It is not something by which I am prepared to stand or fall now, in this mortal life, but on which I am prepared to bet my immortal soul and my destiny.

There are two things to note so far: first, that if I want to make this sort of statement, that there are some questions of conduct that are more important than life itself; things it is better to be dead than to do (and quite a lot of people, not all of them Christians, would want to make statements of that sort); then to use the language of eschatology is certainly one of the handiest ways to do it. It may not be the only possible way to do it, but if I want myself readily to be understood, it is decidedly a very direct way to do it.

95

The second thing to note is that I can use this sort of language, and make it sound convincing, without taking it literally at all. I spoke above about a matter 'on which I am prepared to bet my immortal soul'. Now I should not like to be pressed on the precise meaning to be attached to a phrase like 'immortal soul'. I find it hard to subscribe to anything resembling the traditional catholic idea of the soul. To me, a phrase like that is just a manner of speaking, but it's a manner of speaking that still carries a good deal of emotive force.

Likewise, I would not like anyone to imagine that I entertained any crudely literalistic ideas about heaven and hell, or anticipated a last day in which God will appear, seated on a great white throne, and all the dead of earth, I among them, queueing up to be judged. Yet in spite of that, if I were genuinely being tempted into serious wrong-doing, the question 'How shall I stand before God?' would carry a lot more weight with my conscience than any other argument.

What I am trying to show here is that eschatological language provides a way of asserting the ultimate importance of certain values to which we are attached, and that its usefulness in doing so does not depend on our taking it literally.

That last sentence contains a giveaway phrase which indicates just why it is that eschatological language has these possibilities. Why did I say *'ultimate* importance'? 'Ultimate', literally, means 'last'. Eschatological language is useful because it is a convenient way of indicating what *in the last resort* matters most to us; what *in the final analysis* we are prepared to stand or fall by; what *at the end of the day* we set most store by. The italicized words demonstrate, I think, just how naturally we resort to the language of finality when we attempt to express intensity of conviction. What is 'ultimate' in the moral sense is not necessarily ultimate in the temporal sense. One doesn't need to be an expert in analysing language to see the difference between the two senses of the word. But there is no denying that the human mind very easily translates one into the other. If one wishes to give one's talk about one's ultimate concerns any force, to give it an impact on the imagination, then to use the language of finality is a quick and convenient way to do so.

2. Now there is one fairly clear reason why we find this transition from 'last', in the temporal sense, to 'ultimate', in the moral sense, so easy to make. Eschatological language is the language of crisis, and it is a fact of experience that a crisis has a way of revealing people's true character. It is also apt to reveal their true values, what they really stand for.

This is the sort of point the existentialists make, too, in their own way. The ultimate crisis, they are inclined to point out, is death. When a man stops hood-winking himself; when he stops pretending or acting as if he was here for ever; when he accepts his status as 'one who must die', what then does he consider important? What at that stage does he set his affections on? This kind of language is very close to that of eschatology. It certainly makes use of an insight that is fundamental to eschatology, too, that the consciousness of an end produces an abrupt change of perspective.

If I were told that I had only six months to live, there are some things about which I would suddenly stop bothering. There are others about which I should be bothering a lot more than I now am. If I were given only a week to live this drastic change in my perspective would be different again. To think eschatologically is to put oneself in this sort of situation. It is to think in the manner of someone facing this sort of crisis. Eschatology demands that, faced with any moral decision, we take it as a man who is to face the firing squad at dawn tomorrow.

Why should this be a profitable thing to do? If I knew that I was to face the firing squad at dawn tomorrow I should no doubt be very apprehensive about the execution itself, but there are some things of which I should no longer be afraid. And I am convinced that many of the things that would cease to matter, there on the threshold of eternity, are things which ought not to matter to a Christian anyway. This is one chief value of crisis language. It reminds us of what we know to be true, but don't act upon, that however far we may be from the firing squad we are already on the threshold of eternity.

I have said that the existentialists make the same point very well. It is made equally well, on occasion, in rabbinic Judaism. Rabbi Eliezer ben Hyrcanus is reported to have uttered the following advice: 'Let the honour of thy fellow be as dear to thee as thine own, be not easily moved to anger, *and repent one day before thy death.*' This has all the delicacy, the irony, the two-edgedness of the best rabbinic aphorisms. Totally unlike the characteristic hyperbole of Jesus, it relies on the soft sell to get its effects. Such a comforting invitation to leave repentance till the eleventh hour! But who knows the day of his death? How do you know that it is not, even now, the eleventh hour? Under the innocent exterior of that saying is the same forceful demand that one meets again and again in the gospels, to repent *now*, while there is time, and to live as men who any moment might be called to judgment.

This saying brings out another feature of the language of crisis. Not only does the crisis, or the consciousness of an end, bring about a re-ordering of our values, but it

98

imparts a sense of urgency. If one merely wants to suggest the advisability of getting our priorities sorted out, one doesn't need to use crisis language; but if one wants to suggest that it is vital to get them sorted out *now*, then crisis language is the language to which one naturally turns.

But all we have done so far under this heading is to show that eschatological language is a species of crisis language, and that though it can make certain points very well, other kinds of crisis language may be equally effective. Existential language may be strongly reminiscent of eschatological language at times, but it isn't eschatological. It lacks some of the main premises of eschatology. Yet, as we have seen, it may convey the same ideas and convey them very powerfully. The rabbinic saying which was quoted above isn't eschatological either. There may be some eschatological thinking implicit in it. Its author is probably taking for granted some sort of divine judgment. But it isn't explicitly eschatological, and anyone reading it who didn't start by sharing its author's presuppositions about the world to come could still find it meaningful and moving.

So crisis language, language that faces us with the fact that we have only one life to live, one lifetime in which to choose, is useful, perhaps essential, if we are to express both the urgency of the moral demand and the kind of moral perspective which is desirable — but why *eschatological* language particularly? What does eschatology say that existentialism doesn't say, or that other kinds of crisis language don't say?

What existentialism does, and what other kinds of crisis language almost inevitably do, is to *individualize* the crisis. They convey very well the notion that *I* am under judgment; that *I* am living on borrowed time; that

99

the choice *for me* is of surpassing urgency. But it is always *for me* and for *my* eternal destiny that the decision is important. Christian eschatology is vitally different. For the New Testament it is the world, the cosmos which is under judgment; the earth itself is temporary, 'the whole *schema* of the world' (the entire set-up, one might say) 'is passing away' (I Cor. 7.31); the entire race of men has only this once to work out its destiny. This is something which Christian eschatology says which other kinds of crisis language don't usually manage to say, and it seems to me that if ever there was a time in the history of mankind when such a message was relevant, it is now. Our whole civilization must settle its moral priorities in the light of the fact that any day it might be called to judgment.

But isn't all this rather unrealistic? Or, to be blunter, doesn't it amount to a sort of self-deception? Can I, knowing perfectly well that I am not going to face the firing squad at dawn tomorrow, live as if I were? Even granted that it is true that a Christian's attitude to the good things of this life approximates to that of a man who is about to leave it, can I con myself into taking up this attitude by presenting myself with an imaginary crisis?

Furthermore, even though it may be true up to a point that Christian values are, as it were, crisis values, is this all that can be said about them? Is this not true *only* 'up to a point'? If I act *consistently* as if I stood in a crisis situation, am I not likely to make some rather ridiculous decisions?

These questions have, in a sense, already been answered, but they must be answered again explicitly here, for they are crucial to the whole attempt to re-present our faith in eschatological terms.

The answer to the first is that the crisis is not

imaginary. On the individual level my own mortality *is* one of the most important facts (and undoubtedly one of the most assured facts) which I must take account of when making my moral decisions. When I decide what it is that I live for; when I decide what to set my heart on; when I decide what priority to give to the variety of good things that the world offers me, it is very material to my decision that I should remember that it is a once-for-all decision; that I have only this one lifetime to dispose of.

It is also extremely relevant to my decision that this one lifetime is itself not entirely under my control. In some very important as well as in a number of quite trivial respects I am not my own master. I cannot, by thinking about it, add one cubit to my stature or make one hair of my head white or black. Above all, I cannot determine how long my life will be. I must not, like the man in the parable, make my plans in contempt of the fact that this very night my soul might be required of me.

The knowledge of my own mortality may not, in the narrow sense of the word, constitute a crisis, but it is the kind of knowledge which the crisis language of eschatology reminds us of, and it is not being unrealistic in doing so, but the very reverse. It is the rich fool who is the unrealistic one, the man who cannot see the angel of death standing behind his chair.

On the corporate or cosmic level, as I have earlier tried to show, the crisis language of eschatology is again realistic. What constitutes the crisis is not the imminence of an end, but the possibility of an end. It is, if you like, a *latent* crisis in which we live. We live, if not in crisis, on the edge of crisis. To make realistic decisions we must remain alive to that fact.

As to the second question, I have at a number of

points admitted, and here freely admit, indeed assert, once more, that this 'crisis attitude' cannot be consistently carried through into all departments of life. We cannot, and must not behave *in all respects* as if we were about to die, or about to witness the end of the world. The New Testament itself does not support us if we do. The thoroughgoing adventist, who thinks he has calculated the date of the Lord's return and thinks it will be soon; who gives up his job and retires to watch and pray; this man is as much a man of unbelief as the rich fool is. They both fall into the same error. They insist on behaving *as if they knew what the future held.* The rich fool (and his is the commoner mistake) forgets that the future holds the possibility of an end. The thoroughgoing adventist forgets that it holds any other possibility. The man of faith does not know what the future holds. He knows that he does not know. He is prepared to face the fact that he does not know and to accept *all* the consequences. Because he has faith in God he does not mind not knowing. He is prepared to act and to plan responsibly in the light of the possibility that his life will go on and his world will go for some time. He accepts with equanimity the possibility that either he or it may end at any time. And if an end comes, he is prepared to face it with cheerfulness and with profound joy.

3. Under the last heading I characterized eschatological language as 'crisis language', and suggested that one reason why it is appropriate or useful is that the crisis has a way of revealing a man's true character. How we act or think in a crisis reveals our true selves. One way in which the crisis achieves this result is by forcing us to take sides.

Human beings in general are congenital fence-sitters. Most of us are uncomfortable on any issue unless we feel ourselves to be somewhere near the middle ground. We dignify our position by saying that we can see both sides of the question; that though we are inclined *this* way, those who are inclined *that* way nevertheless 'have a point'. Put more unkindly, we like to have it both ways. We don't like being too far out of sympathy with anyone or anything, except for those whom we can with relief identify as rank outsiders and on whom we can vent our hatred and contempt without having to feel guilty about it.

Practically all of us who call ourselves Christians feel like this about religion. We want the comforts and advantages of faith, but are anxious not to get *too* far out on a limb in the eyes of the secular world. We wouldn't do anything *extreme*, you understand, anything fanatical; nothing that might give the impression that we are cranks, or anything of that sort. We like to be seen doing things which, though they are Christian enough, we know the world would approve of, see the sense of in its own terms. I sometimes suspect that our rediscovered emphasis on charity; the common insistence that giving money to Christian Aid or to Oxfam is much more important than spending it on the upkeep of antiquated buildings or the running of the church machine, is at least partly due to a feeling which we have taken over from the godless world, that time or money spent on the *purely* religious is really wasted. Religion is all right if it can be seen to justify itself in such tangible ways, but is rather useless, and perhaps even pernicious, otherwise. So we emphasize this fashionable, secular-looking aspect of our gospel, or find ourselves attracted by various radicalisms which seem to offer us the possibility of a compromise, a half-way house, or at least a stepping stone, a place to stand, however precariously, between traditional religion and

103

godless materialism, but which frighteningly often end (or even begin) by devaluing the purely spiritual life.

I mustn't pursue this line further. It may be a red herring. I brought it in simply to illustrate our devotion to moderation, our propensity for seeing all sides of the question, our reluctance actually to take sides. The crisis forces us to take sides. It makes us come down off the fence. It puts us in the position of having to declare where we really stand.

It is easy to find examples of this sort of crisis. There's a war on. Nobody in his right mind wants it. Nobody wants to take sides. Nobody *wants* to fight. But here it is. It's happened. However ready you may be to see the enemy's point of view, the time for that is over. It's win or lose, kill or be killed now.

It's the revolution. The barricades are up. You can see what the left are fighting for, but you don't like their methods. You can see why the right are resisting. But you don't like their methods. Yet when the chips are down either you're on this side of the barricade or that.

You're an Ulsterman; a moderate of course. Aren't we all? The worst thing that can happen, you think, is civil war. You do everything you can for peace. But if the war comes, either you're a Catholic or a Protestant. And with whatever reluctance you declare yourself, declare yourself you do. For if you don't get up and wave a flag, you will declare by your actions, or your inaction, which side of the fence you have been forced down on. If you're a Catholic will you, however opposed to violence you may be, actually stand up in court and give evidence that you saw who planted the bomb? When it comes to *that* kind of crunch, are there any left wavering?

This is what I mean by the crisis that forces us off the fence. Crisis language insists on the imperative necessity for taking sides, for declaring ourselves. In the New Testament the coming of Christ is the crisis event. His presence leaves men with no alternative but to say where they stand. They have to be either for him or against him, and they reveal their true natures by the decision that they take. This is why the New Testament can use eschatological language to describe the coming of Jesus, why his ministry can be thought of as the beginning of the last times, because it shares the essential characteristic of all crisis events of forcing the issue, of clarifying the decisions to be taken.

4. This simplification of the moral issues is one of the most important aspects of the eschatological perspective. It faces us with clear-cut choices. Most of life is like a vast opinion poll, in which the majority of us are content to be set down in the 'Don't know' column. The crisis denies us the option of the 'don't know' position. It's time to stand up and be counted. Whatever reservations we may still have, we must now say definitively whether we are for or against. This forces us to look to the heart of the problem.

Men of faith, it seems to me, have usually been great takers of sides. The saints have never been much cop at seeing all sides of a question. This is not where their expertise usually lies. Their strength is generally in seeing to the heart of a matter and saying yes or no.

There is an exercise I have sometimes set my students when they study the book of Amos. I ask them to reconstruct Amaziah's reply to Amos (which the Bible itself doesn't, of course, record), to put themselves in Amaziah's place and ask themselves what there was to be said for his position, as the upholder of a state religion, of a sacrificial system, an institutionalized means of procuring forgiveness for the sins that Amos said God was not going to forgive. As an academic

105

exercise it's a very useful one. It helps one to understand both history and theology. But if *Amos* had stopped to think what there was to be said for Amaziah's position there would be no book of Amos, and perhaps no Old Testament. A prophet or a saint is a man who sees things in black and white, while the rest of us pride ourselves on our ability to distinguish between so many shades of grey.

I read an article a few months ago which I wish I had kept. It was about one of those people who in the very early days of Nazism in Germany fell foul of the regime. He was only an ordinary man; a factory worker or a farm worker or something. Not a church leader, or for that matter a leader of any description. He had no following. He had a wife and family, though. He didn't do anything that hit the headlines; anything spectacular. He just said no. And died. And nobody much noticed. And hardly anybody remembered. And that was at a time when the issue of Nazism and what it really was and where it was really going had not become clear enough to shift many churchmen off the fence. There were plenty of reasons, for a while, to live and let live; to see what happened, to see which way things would go. After all, it was a complicated moral and political question. But this man didn't see the complications. He saw, with the simple vision of the simple saint, what it was all about. And he said no, right there at the beginning. And died. They tried to persuade him. His priest tried — and his bishop. They used all the sensible arguments. But he saw things as the saints see, in black and white, and it was only when all was over that the others saw that he had been right.

This is what being a saint means. It means having this clarity of vision, this ruthlessness of moral logic that disregards all special pleading, all so-called 'realism', all reasons of state — that stands up at the beginning and says no.

This is what can be achieved by the eschatological perspective, the crisis mentality. The crisis, the eschaton, reduces the chaos of conflicting loyalties, conflicting values, to one or two very stark choices.

I have used the analogy of the civil war, of the revolution — there is another instructive one, which comes close to not being an analogy at all. It's the situation of the martyr, the Christian under persecution, given the choice of confessing and dying for his faith, or lapsing (as our forefathers put it). One doesn't normally think of the martyr's situation as an enviable one, but in one respect it is. Those of us who live in the world at large, with a future, as we fancy, stretching in front of us; with jobs to do and families to come home to and mortgages to pay and the complicated business of civilized life to cope with, have so many things to think about. Almost any moral issue you care to name, public or private, has got so many sides to it, so many complicating factors. In almost any real life situation almost any course of action can be plausibly defended as the right one. We are quite accustomed to find honourable, and sincere, and Christian men and women lining up on opposite sides of the burning issues of the day, and each side getting very heated about it and feeling very strongly that it is right. There are so many and such very good reasons why abortion on demand should not be allowed, and so many and such very good reasons why it should. There are so many reasons why contraceptives should not be too freely available; and so many why they should be made as freely available as possible. There are so many good reasons for devoting my income to this rather than that; and so many equally good ones for devoting it to that rather than this. I ought, I positively and morally speaking ought, to spend more of my time on x. But equally, I positively and morally speaking must spend more of it on y. The result of all these complications is that whatever choice one makes, one feels guilty about it.

The prospective martyr is spared all this. All the issues of life and death resolve themselves for him to one. And in the ordinary way (if you can speak of facing martyrdom 'in the ordinary way') he hasn't any doubts about what his decision ought to be. True, he may not have the courage for it. True, his faith, or his self-control, or his capacity for endurance, may not be up to the job. But he hasn't any doubts about what the job is. All the greys of the moral life of the world the rest of us inhabit resolve themselves to this one black and white demand, to confess and die.

I never used to be able to understand those enthusiasts of the early Christian centuries (their more balanced-minded brethren condemned them for it) who went out *looking* for martyrdom. But nowadays I begin *just* to see the appeal.

But leaving aside these curious characters who actually sought martyrdom, the attitude of Christian orthodoxy itself to the subject was interesting and significant enough. The proper way, the accepted way to become a Christian was in those days to become first a catechumen, i.e. to put oneself under instruction. After that, one made a public profession of faith, was baptized, and came to the sacrament of the eucharist. These things, instruction, profession of faith, baptism, were the essentials of entry into the Christian church. 'Essentials'? The martyr was excused them all. Instruction or no instruction, he understood enough. Profession of faith? How better to make it than the way he had chosen? Baptism? His was the baptism of blood.

108

What he did counted for everything. The martyr could step from paganism to the throne of God in a single leap. Presented, once for all time, with Christ's demand in its most radical form, he had by taking one decision taken all decisions. The process of justification, sanctification and redemption which takes the rest of us a lifetime and maybe more, he telescoped into a transmuting instant of agony and glory.

What the exigencies of the hour did for the martyr the eschatological perspective does for us all. For the Christian, seeing himself as living at the end, any choice can present itself with the clarity and simplicity of the demand laid before the martyr. Any or every moment can be the moment of truth.

5. This, it seems to me, is the main value of the language of eschatology. It is capable of radicalizing any or every choice. In doing so it can reduce the decisions of life to these great simplicities. And above all, it focuses interest and significance on to certain crucial issues by which everything else stands or falls.

This is a thread which runs through the New Testament, whether it is using eschatological language or not. It insists on pinning everything on what I am calling, rather crudely, certain 'crunch' issues. That is to say, there are certain issues by which a man is judged, because it is by his stand on these issues that he declares which side he is on. Or sometimes, it isn't so much a matter of taking his stand on certain issues — it is something less momentous-looking than that. He hardly needs to do anything as serious as to 'take a stand'. He often appears to be judged by a mere gesture that he makes, or by an almost casual word.

The woman who was a sinner anoints Jesus's feet. She must have been a very emotional girl. It is an extravagant gesture and, most of us would say, a somewhat embarassing one. And what sort of girl is she, anyway? Not a nice girl, certainly. Her sins, as Jesus himself acknowledges, 'were many'. But the gesture, awkward as some of us would take it to be, counts. It counts for everything. It counts because it is a declaration of allegiance. Nice girl or not, she's on the right side, *our* side. And Simon the Pharisee, who didn't think much of Jesus's criteria of judgment, had made a declaration, too. He had made it just as certainly in what he didn't do. He was probably a very good man, by most of the standards that *we* should apply. He fell down on one test, but it happened to be the one that mattered.

Jesus's tests sometimes remind one of those aptitude tests they used to give people in the army, and which I think the careers advisers in schools and universities sometimes use. They give you a few puzzles to do or ask you a long list of questions and then come up with the information that you ought to be a plumber or an accountant or a surgeon or something. But it is always a mystery to the layman what the questions they ask and the puzzles they set have got to do with the problem they are supposed to be solving, and how they get from the answers you give to the advice they offer. Somehow or other the puzzles and the questions must contain some sort of give-away, betraying to the skilled psychologist the kind of person you really are and the skills you possess or are capable of acquiring.

I'm not suggesting that Jesus's criteria are as arbitrary as those in the aptitude tests often look. But I suspect they work in the same way. By one's performance in certain crucial situations one reveals where one really stands. An instinctive, trivial act, like the offer of a cup of cold water, declares one's allegiance as surely as if one had waved a flag. A word lightly spoken, an aside, a joke, is taken as a password, to heaven or hell.

110

Look at the thief on the cross. He wasn't a nice man either. He doesn't exactly make a big confession of faith. Half ironically, it seems, he turns to Jesus (doesn't even call him 'Lord', just 'Jesus'). 'Jesus,' he says, 'remember me when you get to your kingdom.' 'Jesus, remember me.' Never did a man get into heaven on less than that. But it's enough. He's in! He didn't know it, but he happened to say the password.

Does all this make any kind of sense at all? Yes, it does, because there are situations in life in which we do judge people in exactly this way, and in which it is reasonable to do so. I heard of an American ex-soldier the other day who said that he 'wished the war was back. Because then you knew the good guys from the bad guys.' I know what he meant. War has a certain simplicity. You know the good guys from the bad guys from the colour of their uniforms and the shape of their hats. In a war the good guys are the ones who are on your side, and the bad guys are the ones that aren't. There's no arguing with that. How do you know the other fellows are bad guys? They must be; they're trying to kill you, aren't they? And this other chap, the one with the same shaped hat as you, how do you know he's a good guy? You know nothing about him. You've never met him before. You don't know what his background is; what his job was, or his father's job; whether he's ever been to jail; whether you've any interests in common; yet in a tight spot you would trust him with your life and he'd trust you with his. Does this make sense? In a war, yes. He's wearing the right hat, isn't he? And whatever kind of a bastard he may be under that hat, for present purposes he has to count as a good guy.

Notice how naturally, when we look for illustrations, the crisis situation, the war, springs to mind. The

111

situation in the New Testament is like that. Some of the people on our side are very odd people indeed, prostitutes, people with criminal records, shady characters of all sorts. And we know very well that there are some very nice people (as most of the Pharisees were) on the other side. But there's no time to worry about that, there's a war on. Nice chaps or not, if they've decided for the other side they're the enemy. This is the message of the New Testament: the crisis *is here*. Get on the right side now. You don't have to be a saint. You only have to be on the side where the saints are.

If you're on the right side you can afford to get a lot of other things wrong. Similarly, if you come up to scratch in the crisis, at the crucial point, you can afford to fail for most of the rest of the time. This, too, makes sense in terms of many familiar situations.

Let us illustrate from another crisis situation. The dramatic society is putting on a play. Every old hand will tell you that a rotten dress rehearsal is a very hopeful sign — and that if the dress rehearsal goes like a charm then the real thing will be a flop. The most marvellous rehearsals in dramatic history won't do anything for the company's reputation if it all falls flat for the audience. And the most disastrous dress rehearsal ever won't matter a scrap, if it's all right on the night. The production stands or falls *solely* by what it's like on the night.

Another analogy — a game of tennis. If you know anything at all about tennis you'll know that a lot of the interest of the game is in the way it is scored. Some points are much more significant than others. It doesn't matter how many points you score if you can't hit winners on the ones that matter most. Years ago, long before my time, there was a famous match between Bill Tilden and Henri Cochet. Tilden was a big chap, about

112

six feet six, and Cochet was a tiny little Frenchman. Tilden was all over him. He took the first two sets (in a five set match) and in the third set he got to 5 − 0 and forty love in the sixth game. Now you can't get a stronger position than that. Three match points to start with! One by one Tilden lost them. Cochet went on and took the game. Then he held on to five games all and ended by taking the set. Tilden, by now thoroughly demoralized, lost the last two sets and the match. It doesn't matter how superior your performance. It doesn't matter how many ace services you serve or how many ungettable smashes you send back. If you can't clinch the match point when it comes, it was all a waste of time.

It's a bit like one of those quizzes they used to have on television (do they still?) where the victim is asked a series of questions, and he has to get each one right before he can go on to the next. The little questions are really only opportunities to get asked the big one. If you fail on the sixty-four thousand dollar question you get nothing at all.

The Pharisees did quite well on the little questions. They looked all set for the jackpot. But when it came to the big question they said, 'Crucify'. It was the wrong answer.

In the gospels the crunch comes when people are faced with Jesus. 'This is the crisis,' says St John, 'that light is come into the world' (John 3.19). Everyone stands or falls by this single criterion: What attitude does he take up to Jesus? St Paul puts the same point in a way that at first sight is rather different. In that famous chapter of I Corinthians 13, he says that the crunch issue is whether you love. It doesn't matter what else you do; what miracles you work, how marvellous a preacher you are; how generous you are with your time,

113

your money, your lifeblood even; if you fail at this one point it's all quite futile. And if you do love, then it doesn't matter what else you've done. Your sins, which may be many, are forgiven.

Matthew 25, the parable of the sheep and the goats, demonstrates neatly that these are not different tests after all, but the same test. To respond with love and to say yes to Jesus are not different things, but the same thing.

Matthew 25 makes a further point, that the declaration of allegiance isn't necessarily a conscious one. Simon the Pharisee, refusing the normal courtesies, the woman who was a sinner anointing Jesus's feet, the thief saying 'Remember me', the people offering the cup of cold water to the least of his brethren, none of these *know* they're standing up and being counted. But they are.

Are all these people, then, 'believers'? Maybe. Maybe not. What matters is that *they count as believers.* To rephrase something I said earlier, whether they are believers or not isn't the thing that matters most. They are on the side where the believers are.

Once more, let us admit that much of this can be said without eschatological language. Nevertheless, if one wants to say it forcefully and convincingly, eschatological language is the sort that comes most readily to mind. The parable of the sheep and the goats is very much an eschatological parable, as are most of the other 'parables of the kingdom'. St Paul tries to say some of the same things in non-eschatological language, by elaborating his doctrine of justification by faith. Both St Paul and the parable are insisting that if you get it right at the one point that matters, you can afford to get it wrong at all the others. And if you get it wrong at the point that matters, it doesn't help you to have got it right at all the others. If, when it comes to the crunch, you make the response of love and faith, then that counts for everything. If you fail to make it, all else goes for nothing. But the doctrine of justification by faith has caused endless trouble because it is horribly difficult to state convincingly. It almost inevitably makes God sound arbitrary and unfair. The eschatological language of the parable puts it in a way anyone can understand and say yes to.

The doctrine of justification by faith makes God sound like a judge who lets the guilty criminal go free. Very nice, no doubt, for the criminal concerned, but hardly what the judge is there for. This fails to convince because this situation, the law court situation, does not strike us as one in which this sort of clemency is appropriate. The eschatological parables convince because they use a different analogy, the analogy of the crisis situation. And in this situation the behaviour postulated of God does make sense, because in a crisis men do judge and are judged by these very simple criteria — What hat is he wearing? What flag does he wave. Whose side is he on?

The popular traditional image of judgment after death (the one that figures in all those jokes about the man who died and went to heaven) is the account-book image. The picture is always of St Peter standing at the gate, with the recording angel at his elbow totting up the total of good deeds and bad deeds, striking a balance and deciding the issue according to whether the applicant is in debit or credit. If we think in terms of this sort of image, then there is no justification for the sinner without cooking the books. To change the image slightly, it is like a game of rugby, in which every point scored goes on the tally, and the side with the most points at the end has won the game. But the New Testament isn't thinking in terms of this sort of scoring system. A better sporting analogy is the sort of game where right up to the end anyone *could* win; where the apparent winner could lose everything on the last throw of the dice, and the apparent loser come through.

There are two criticisms to be made of this kind of language, this way of stating the issue. They are not unrelated. The first is that it is still, even stated as I have stated it, an unfair way of doing things. Why *should* so much weight be placed on particular decisions? Why *should* men stand or fall by a single brief test? The second is that such a way of representing divine judgment is a very. dangerous one. If all that matters is that I should get it right at the crucial point, why should I even try to get it right anywhere else? If it is only on my answers to the big question that I am to be judged, why should I bother about the little ones at all?

The answer to both objections is the same. The crucial issues by which we stand or fall are not really unrelated to the rest of life, though they may look as if they are. How I act in the crisis reveals the kind of person I have been *all along*. If I treat the little questions too lightly, I may never be offered the big one. No doubt the production will be judged solely by what it's like on the night, but this doesn't mean that we can dispense with rehearsals altogether. If I let the little opportunities go, complacently feeling that I can always make sure of the big ones, I may find when the big ones come along that I am no longer the kind of person who can rise to them. I may put off repentance, knowing that the eleventh hour will be soon enough. But how do I know which *is* the eleventh hour?

We miss the point of New Testament eschatology if we forget that this sort of postponement is the very thing it won't allow. When the New Testament talks about the day of judgment, it isn't talking of something

116

far off in the future. When it talks about the crisis, it means the crisis in front of us *now*. The question that faces me *at this minute* is the sixty-four thousand dollar question. The chance in front of me *at the moment* is the last chance. This *is* the eleventh hour. This is the whole essence of the matter: the New Testament changes our whole perspective on the future by stating the awful fact: *the day of judgment is today.*